"Often we are not content; som[...] need help with contentment, a[...] friendly, funny, and easy to rea[...] cal, and Christ centered, drawing as readily from the Puritans as contemporary culture. God spoke to my heart through *The Greener Grass Conspiracy*. Don't be content not to read it."

Randy Alcorn, best-selling author, *The Goodness of God* and *Deception*; founder and director of Eternal Perspective Ministries

"This book should be titled, 'how to be happy.' Not the superficial, frivolous, world-saturated happiness either. No, the soul-quenching, perspective-shaping type flowing from springs of gospel contentment. Stephen Altrogge has found the source and invites us to come and satisfy our thirst. Get this book, drink deeply, and be happy."

Dave Harvey, author, *Rescuing Ambition*; Church Planting and Church Care, Sovereign Grace Ministries

"Stephen Altrogge skillfully polishes off the rare jewel of Christian contentment collecting dust for generations and lets it shine brightly to a new generation of gospel people whose cluttered and discontented hearts long for less to live with and more to live for. His timeless insights are most timely. I highly recommend it!"

Tom Nelson, Senior Pastor, Christ Community Church, Leawood, Kansas

"We crave the other grass when Christ has given us the lushest, all-satisfying plains of hope and joy. With humor and grit, and written within the crucible of suffering, Altrogge exposes and scorches these discontented dreams by magnifying how rich we are in Christ."

Eric C. Redmond, Senior Pastor, Reformation Alive Baptist Church, Temple Hills, Maryland

THE GREENER GRASS CONSPIRACY

THE
GREENER GRASS CONSPIRACY

Finding Contentment on Your Side of the Fence

STEPHEN ALTROGGE

WHEATON, ILLINOIS

First printing 2010

Printed in the United States of America

Italics in biblical quotes indicate emphasis added.

Scripture quotations are from the ESV® Bible (*The Holy Bible, English Standard Version*®), copyright © 2001 by Crossway. Used by permission. All rights reserved.

Scripture indicated as from NIV is taken from *The Holy Bible, New International Version*®. Copyright © 1973, 1978, 1984 by Biblica. Used by permission of Zondervan. All rights reserved. The "NIV" and "New International Version" trademarks are registered in the United States Patent and Trademark Office by Biblica. Use of either trademark requires the permission of Biblica.

ISBN-13: 978-1-4335-2115-7
ISBN-10: 1-4335-2115-6
PDF ISBN: 978-1-4335-2116-4
Mobipocket ISBN: 978-1-4335-2117-1
ePub ISBN: 978-1-4335-2128-7

Library of Congress Cataloging-in-Publication Data
Altrogge, Stephen, 1982–
   The greener grass conspiracy : finding contentment on your side
of the fence / Stephen Altrogge.
      p. cm.
Includes bibliographical references.
   ISBN 978-1-4335-2115-7 (tpb)
   1. Contentment—Biblical teaching. 2. Contentment—Religious aspects—
Christianity. I. Title.
BS680.C64A48   2011
241'.4—dc22   2010019841

Crossway is a publishing ministry of Good News Publishers.

VP		20	19	18	17	16	15	14	13	12	11
14	13	12	11	10	9	8	7	6	5	4	3	2	1

To my two princesses,
Charis and Ella

CONTENTS

THE CONSPIRACY

I've never believed in conspiracies. Lee Harvey Oswald acted alone. The United States government is not hiding evidence of extraterrestrial life in Area 51. Men really did walk on the moon. George W. Bush is not in league with the Taliban. The Three Mile Island nuclear meltdown was not caused by Communist river pirates hired by Walt Disney. Donald Trump's hair is not the result of experimental government testing (although I could be persuaded).

And to be honest, conspiracy theorists don't do much to help their case. They wear tinfoil helmets and launch into wild-eyed, spittle-producing tirades against the national government, accusing it of everything from price fixing to water supply contamination. They form clubs, complete with newsletters, secret handshakes, and regular attempts to make contact with alien life. They don't put money in banks because banks are obviously a part of the conspiracy, whatever that conspiracy may be. And unless you can pick fourteen separate dead bolts, you won't be able to break into their house. Conspiracy theorists can be downright freaky.[1]

Conspiracy theories have always been the stuff of Harrison Ford movies and Tom Clancy novels, both of which I enjoy. But that's just it: they're fiction. Stories. Legends. Circulated by guys who live with their parents and have too much time on their hands. They're simply too far-fetched to be believable. At least that's what I always thought.

Then I discovered that I was part of a conspiracy—a conspiracy of massive proportions, spanning the entire globe. You're involved in it too, even if you don't know it. No one can escape it, because everyone is a part of it. Go ahead, lock your doors and barricade yourself in the cellar. Stock up on canned goods and cheap paperback novels. Bring out the generator and the bottled water you bought for Y2K. Seal yourself off from the rest of society. Put on your tinfoil helmet. It won't do any good.

And lest you think I'm exaggerating, it gets bigger. Satan is in on the conspiracy. The Prince of Darkness himself has a significant stake in the outcome. This is bigger than international price-fixing and makes Enron look like a fairy tale.

Am I sounding wild-eyed? Is spittle collecting in the corners of my mouth? I speak the truth. I'm not crazy, at least not in the "please pass the tinfoil" kind of way.

Let me bring forth the evidence. Exhibit A: you and me. Do you ever wonder how it's possible to be so blessed and so unhappy at the same time? To live like kings and behave like ungrateful pigs? To have more than any generation in history and yet still crave more? What's wrong with us? Is it the water? Is it cell-phone waves? Did we receive an experimental vaccination in our infancy? Nope. It's the conspiracy.

What is it that I'm ranting about? What exactly is this conspiracy, and who are the masterminds behind this sinister plot? Let me spell it out for you. It's a conspiracy between the world, my heart, and Satan to steal my happiness. These three are plotting and scheming together to make me perpetually discontent. They're stubbornly determined to poison the joy I have in God and to deceive me into believing that I can find happiness somewhere other than God. They want me to dishonor God by gorging on the unsatisfying pleasures of the world instead of finding true joy and satisfaction in Christ.

Everywhere I turn, the world is offering me pleasure. I'm told to buy more things, have more fun, drink more beer, purchase a bigger house, climb the career ladder, get married, stay single, don't think about tomorrow. Happiness is just around the corner, in aisle thirteen at Best Buy. The world makes big, fat promises of immediate pleasure. It flashes its artificially whitened teeth and tells me to enjoy myself. The world lies to me.

Satan joins with the world, whispering lies in my ear, saying that God is holding back from me and doesn't want me to be happy. He tells me that if God really loved me, I wouldn't be sick, or struggle financially, or be single. If God was truly good I wouldn't still be worrying about losing my house. Satan invites me to find satisfaction in something other than God. It doesn't matter if it's pornography or community service, as long as it's not God. Satan is happy as long as I'm not happy in God. Satan slanders God's character and his goodness. Satan lies to me.

My heart doesn't want to be left out of the conspiracy, and so it plays right along with the world and Satan. It tells me that I *need* to have certain things, and I need to have them *now*. I can't be happy unless I get that new television, or salary bump, or house with a nice backyard, or a good night's sleep. My heart persuades me that all my longings for peace and comfort and joy can be satisfied in things other than God. If I have children I'll be happy. If I get married I'll be happy. If I can finally get out of this stupid college I'll be happy. My heart lies to me.

The conspiracy is powerful. Walking into Wal-Mart (or any retail store) is like walking into conspiracy headquarters. As I walk through the store, I'm assaulted from every direction. Fifteen high-definition televisions stand at attention, each one promising outstanding picture quality, superior media experience, and world peace. A box of cereal informs me that I can be slim and heart-healthy if I eat a mere three bowls a day, seven days a week. A high-gloss magazine advertises an article entitled "223 Ways to Be Happier and Get What You Want, without Doing Any Work." Before I entered Wal-Mart I was pretty happy with my life. Now I want more things. The conspiracy is everywhere!

This grand conspiracy of the world, Satan, and my heart is called the Greener Grass Conspiracy. Their objective? To have me always believing that the grass is greener somewhere else, always wishing that things were different, always dreaming of a brighter tomorrow without ever enjoying where God has me today.

This book is not the memoir of a contented man. It's not the poignant reflections of a white-haired guru who has finally figured out the secret to contentment. It's more like sweaty, bloody, hastily scribbled notes from a battlefield. I'm still struggling to escape the sinister fingers of this conspiracy. I'm still waging war against the discontentment that rages in my life. I can see contentment in the distance, like a hazy oasis, but I have to pick my way through a minefield to get there. I'm not the contented man God wants me to be, but I'm fighting to get there.

I'm writing this book in the hope that you'll join me in the fight.

1

WHY AM I SO UNHAPPY?

I had a very unhappy childhood.

But not in the way you're thinking. I had the best parents in the world who loved me, showered me with affection, and taught me to follow Jesus. I lived in a wonderful house, ate between three and six square meals a day, got along well with my siblings, and had a dog named Sparky who was very good except when he lost control of his bowels in the house.

My unhappiness stemmed from a game. Again, don't misunderstand me. I wasn't into locking myself in my parents' basement, turning on a black light, and playing a life-consuming role-playing game. No, this game was far worse in many ways. It was called the "if only" game. I'm not sure when I started playing it. Maybe I was born playing it.

Here's how the "if only" game works. Think about what would make you happy. I mean really, freakishly, "I can't believe this is happening to me" happy. What do you obsess about, dream about, desperately hope for?

Now put the words "if only" in front of that dream. *If only I could get married, then I would be happy. If only I could get the job promotion that would get me out of cubicle-land and into the corner office, then I would be satisfied. If only my wife weren't sick so often . . . if only my son would start respecting me . . . if only my budget wasn't so tight, then I'd have peace, joy, contentment, and some sleep at night.*

Once you've identified your "if only" dream, invest all your hopes in that dream and spend hours thinking and praying about it.

Put all your hopes for life and happiness into that dream. Imagine how happy you'll finally be when that dream is fulfilled.

Most people are good at playing the "if only" game. The only problem is, you can never win. I've been playing it for years and haven't won once. But that doesn't stop me. I just keep playing, like a wheezy old man hooked on scratch lottery cards. My life has been a succession of if onlys.

I was homeschooled throughout grade school and high school. I never wore a powder blue tux to the prom, never played varsity football, never dismantled a debate team opponent, never traded punches with an oversized kid named Butch, and never built a giant, foam solar system. I was valedictorian of my class, but I also *was* my class. By the time twelfth grade rolled around I was ready for college.

College fulfilled all my wildest dreams. For two days. Then I made some unpleasant discoveries. I discovered that I wasn't a big fan of memorizing the names of eighteenth-century composers. I discovered that I enjoyed writing ten-page papers like I enjoyed getting tetanus shots. I discovered that some professors were as interesting as shredded wheat and that these professors always had a mandatory attendance policy.

By the end of the first week I was ready for the weekend. By the end of the first year I was ready to get out into the real world. College, just like high school, had failed to deliver.

It turned out that the real world wouldn't come through either. It's hard to get jazzed about sitting in a concrete gray cubicle all day. Every day.

When I was single I desperately wanted to get married. Then I married the most wonderful woman in the world and had a daughter who was cuter than a bucket of puppies. But I still don't own a house. And let me tell you, when I own a house I'll finally be happy. I'm sure of it. I'll sit in my overstuffed recliner, have children playing at my feet, a fire warming my toes, and a dog fetching the latest edition of *Sports Illustrated* (okay, scratch the dog).

Do you get the picture? I've been a discontented person for much of my life, always waiting for that next event/person/place/technological gadget that would fulfill the deepest desires of my heart. Can you relate? My guess is that you can.

I AM MY WORST ENEMY

So what exactly is the problem? Why are so many people so unhappy in so many different circumstances? Why are so many *Christians*, who supposedly have the joy, joy, joy, joy down in their hearts, so *not* joyful?

At first glance it would seem that circumstances are to blame. Can you blame a guy for being unhappy when he hasn't had steady work for six months and he might lose his home? You wouldn't think so, until you meet the six-figure Christian businessman who hates his job and is just hanging on until retirement. The twenty-something single woman doesn't think she can be happy until she gets married and has children. But the thirty-something housewife with four kids can barely make it through the week without collapsing in a trembling heap of exhaustion. Circumstances aren't to blame. There's something much more sinister at work.

That something is my sinful, discontented heart. Jesus spelled it out in Mark 7:21–23 when he said, "For from within, out of the heart of man, come evil thoughts, sexual immorality, theft, murder, adultery, coveting, wickedness, deceit, sensuality, envy, slander, pride, foolishness. All these evil things come from within, and they defile a person." The problem is me. I am my own worst enemy. The raging, covetous, discontented desires come from within. They're not the product of my circumstances, and the desires won't be satisfied when circumstances change.

John Calvin nailed it when he said, "Man's nature, so to speak, is a perpetual factory of idols."[1] In the original context, Calvin was referring to man's constant desire to make an image for God, but his point is applicable nonetheless. Our hearts are raging idol factories, constantly creating new idols for us to worship. These aren't golden, tribal native, "please send the rain, here's a bloody goat" idols. The idols we manufacture are more subtle and dangerous.

First it's marriage. We dream about meeting that perfect someone—a person who likes long walks and French poetry and is kind toward animals and strangers alike. Or at least someone who is decent looking and doesn't have a criminal record. Finally, after years of yearning, the wedding day arrives. But the idol factory doesn't shut down after the wedding day. As soon as the marriage god is appeased, the factory belches forth the idol of a new house. Then it's a new car, an end-of-year bonus, and a sweet retirement package. There's no downtime, no coffee break, no union strike in the factory of our hearts. They are constantly churning, constantly stirring up discontentment, constantly producing new idols.

James 4:1–3 puts it this way:

> What causes quarrels and what causes fights among you? Is it not this, that your passions are at war within you? You desire and do not have, so you murder. You covet and cannot obtain, so you fight and quarrel. You do not have, because you do not ask. You ask and do not receive, because you ask wrongly, to spend it on your passions.

In the original context, James was addressing the cause of fights and quarrels, but I think James would give the same instruction to those who are discontent. Why are we discontent? Because we're at war.

The war starts with a desire. Our hearts latch on to a person, ministry opportunity, car, promotion, house, or anything else. This thing becomes the object of our affections. We want it, need it, dream about it, feel with every fiber of our being that we must have it. Life begins to orbit around this object of our affections.

Then "catastrophe" strikes. The dream promotion is handed to someone else. A relationship never materializes. Our desires are thwarted, and we don't get what we want.

When we don't get what we so desperately want, we throw the adult version of a temper tantrum. Our passions rage within us. We become angry at God and discontent with life. We grumble and complain, and happiness appears to be out of reach. We become a casualty of war.

SHUTTING DOWN THE FACTORY

So is there any hope for raging discontents like me? Can the circus of discontentment in my heart ever be stopped? Thankfully, it can. In Philippians 4:11–12 the apostle Paul said, "Not that I am speaking of being in need, for I have learned in whatever situation I am to be content. I know how to be brought low, and I know how to abound. In any and every circumstance, I have learned the secret of facing plenty and hunger, abundance and need."

These words should startle us and cause us to catch our breath. Paul says that he has learned to be content in *every* situation. Not just happy, comfortable, "why, yes, I will have another latte" situations. Every situation.

Paul could find contentment in any season and any circumstance. He knew how to be brought low, and few people were brought lower than Paul. He was thrown into filthy prisons, savagely beaten with rods, stoned within a breath of death, whipped until his back was a bloody, dripping mess, driven out of cities, betrayed by friends, and shipwrecked on multiple occasions. In the midst of all this, Paul found contentment. The difficulties faced by Paul make my life look like a Boy Scout campout.

Paul also knew how to be content in the midst of prosperity. Prosperity and contentment don't always go together. In fact, they rarely do. Rich people are unhappy just like everyone else. Members of the yacht club need to learn contentment too.

In 1 Timothy 6:6 Paul says of contentment, "Now there is great gain in godliness with contentment." False teachers were invading Timothy's church and telling people that if they were godly they would also be rich, that if they followed Jesus, they would get their Lexus chariot or Rolex sundial or whatever it was they wanted. But Paul won't have any of that nonsense. He says that following Jesus isn't a get-rich-quick scheme. If you follow Jesus, you will have every *spiritual* need met. Forgiveness, adoption, spiritual strength, everything. And if we have all our spiritual needs met *and* are content with what we have, that is *great* gain. If we have every spiritual need met and are content with what we have, what more could we want? We have everything we need for joy. Following a Jesus genie who gives us whatever we want is not great gain. Contentment is great gain.

If you need any further motivation to pursue contentment, there you have it. Godliness + Contentment = Great Gain. I'm into gain. And when God himself, speaking through the Scriptures, says that something is *great* gain, we need to pay close attention.

All of this raises one enormous, potentially life-altering question: What is the secret to contentment? We will be exploring that question for the remainder of this book. Buckle your seat belts.

STOP—THINK—DO

1. Do you ever find yourself playing the "if only" game? What's your current "if only" dream?

2. Do you ever find yourself believing that circumstances are the cause of all your unhappiness? How does Mark 7:21–23 correct that idea?

3. What does it mean that each person's heart is "a perpetual factory of idols"? How have you seen this at work in your own life?

4. Write the word *contentment* on a piece of paper. Underneath write all the other words that you associate with contentment. Based on what you've written, what is your concept of contentment? Does it seem valuable to you?

5. What keeps you from seeing contentment as "great gain"?

2

I'M NOT THE CENTER OF THE UNIVERSE

Remember Copernicus? Yeah, that's the one. The medieval scientist who had the audacity to claim that the earth was *not* the center of the universe. If I had lived during his day, I don't think we would have been good friends. I don't think we would have drunk coffee together, or joined fantasy football leagues together, or discussed the finer points of grilling meat together. I don't think I would have liked Copernicus.

Why? Because he challenged an idea that I'm very fond of—that earth, and in turn humans, are at the center of the universe. Now, before you send angry letters to my mother, demanding to know what she taught me in school, let me explain. I know that the sun is at the center of the solar system and that the earth rotates around the sun and that the earth is just a tiny speck in an unbelievably large universe. But that doesn't mean that I have to like it.

You see, most days I live according to very anti-Copernican principles. I live as though Planet Stephen is at the center of the universe and as though all things should orbit around Planet Stephen. Planet Stephen occupies my thoughts, and I'm eager to discover more ways to make Planet Stephen happy. If someone or something happens to interrupt the orbital path of Planet Stephen, an angry collision will likely result.

If this were purely a scientific matter, I wouldn't be too concerned. But it's not. In all honesty I really do live most days as though

I were the center of the universe. I want each day to unfold in such a way that I receive maximum joy and happiness. I want all the circumstances and people in my life to contribute to my happiness. When something interrupts my wonderful plan for my life, such as a crying baby at 2:00 A.M. or a sinus infection, I'm unhappy because this is my world and these kinds of things shouldn't happen in my world. I don't actually speak those words, but every day I'm tempted to believe them, live by them, and treat others according to them. And I don't think that I'm alone in this temptation. Each of us is tempted to place ourselves at the center of our world.

THE SONG OF CREATION

There's just one slight problem with this line of thinking: it's completely and totally wrong. And sinful. I'm *not* at the center of the universe, and neither are you. In fact, most of the universe takes no notice of us. Psalm 19:1 says, "The heavens declare the glory of God, and the sky above proclaims his handiwork." Right now the heavens are singing about the glory of their Creator. The sky is singing God's anthem and proclaiming his majesty. There are no references to you and me in this song, no verses declaring our praise. The heavens and the earth orbit around God and declare his beauty and his worth. You and I simply aren't in the picture.

But what about angels? Maybe they have something to say about us. Nope. In Isaiah 6:1–3 we read:

> In the year that King Uzziah died I saw the Lord sitting upon a throne, high and lifted up; and the train of his robe filled the temple. Above him stood the seraphim. Each had six wings: with two he covered his face, and with two he covered his feet, and with two he flew. And one called to another and said: "Holy, holy, holy is the LORD of hosts; the whole earth is full of his glory!"

The angels sing one song and only one song: "Holy, holy, holy is the LORD of hosts; the whole earth is full of his glory!" The angels are captivated and mesmerized and overawed by the greatness of God, and in response they tell of God's glory. The angels are not impressed with us. There is no record in Scripture of angels ever singing the praise of a man (with the exception of Christ, who is both man and God). Maybe we're not as important as we thought we were.

Isaiah 40:6–7 further confirms our littleness: "All flesh is grass, and all its beauty is like the flower of the field. The grass withers, the flower fades when the breath of the LORD blows on it; surely the people are grass." If time were a line, you and I would be nothing more than a dot, a pinprick, on the line of history. Billions of people have lived before us. Billions of men and women were born, got married, worked a job, had children, thought they were very important, grew old, and died. And very few of these people are remembered. All the people are like grass that springs up and then quickly withers. My life? Like grass.

In Psalm 8:3–4 David expresses amazement that God would care for us, given his infinite majesty and our very finite littleness. David says, "When I look at your heavens, the work of your fingers, the moon and the stars, which you have set in place, what is man that you are mindful of him, and the son of man that you care for him?"

Have you ever experienced what David is describing? I have on a few occasions. I have as I walked along the beach and stared at the endless expanse of ocean. I have as I lay on my back and stared up at the night sky and the millions of stars scattered across the blackness. I have as I walked through Grand Teton National Park and stared up at monstrous, snow-covered mountains. In those moments I understood and felt that I was not the center of the universe. The mountains and the stars and the beach helped me grasp that there is a great and glorious God who rules over all the earth and who is at the center of the universe. He made the great oceans for his glory. He made the starry blackness as a testimony to his majesty. The grandeur of the mountains points to the grandeur of God. And he made me for his glory as well.

MADE FOR ONE PURPOSE

In Isaiah 43:6–7 we read, "I will say to the north, Give up, and to the south, Do not withhold; bring my sons from afar and my daughters from the end of the earth, everyone who is called by my name, *whom I created for my glory*, whom I formed and made." Our very reason for existence is wrapped in those two verses. Read them again if you need to. We were created for God's glory. In other words, God put you and me on this planet to bring him glory. I exist to display his worth to the world and to show how great God really is. God is at the center of all things, and we exist for him. Not the other way around. Life is not about my ultimate happiness and self-fulfillment. Does God love me? Yes, absolutely. But he doesn't exist for me. Everything exists by God and for God. The universe orbits around God.

Discontentment begins when I start trying to be God. Discontentment happens when I attempt to displace God from his rightful place at the center of the universe. When I think that everything should run according to my plans instead of God's plans. When I forget that God is God and that he is allowed to do with me whatever he wants, whatever will bring him glory. Discontentment results from a big view of myself and a very little view of God.

Contentment is created in the shadow of the majesty of God. I become content when I see and treasure and embrace the glory of God. I find contentment when I grasp the fact that life is not primarily about me and my comfort and my happiness. My soul is satisfied when I stop trying to elbow my way to the center of the universe and instead rejoice in and worship the God who really is at the center of all things.

If I want to be content, I need to get on board with God's plan for my life. I was created to bring him glory and to show his greatness. God shows his glory in different ways through different people. He displays his glory in some people by allowing them to suffer and then gives them incredible amounts of grace in the midst of that suffering. He shows his glory in others by abundantly blessing them and then giving them a heart that overflows with generosity. To some he gives a large family, so that they might raise their children to the glory of God. To others he gives the gift of singleness, so that they might pour all their energies into serving Jesus. God is God, and he will display his glory in us as *he* chooses.

By the grace of God, we must learn to be content in what he chooses. We need to have such a passion for the glory of God that we say, "Lord, glorify yourself in me, however you choose." The apostle Paul had this attitude when he said, "But I do not account my life of any value nor as precious to myself, if only I may finish my course and the ministry that I received from the Lord Jesus, to testify to the gospel of the grace of God" (Acts 20:24). Paul did not count his life of any value or as precious to himself. He was consumed with such a passion to bring God glory through the preaching of the gospel that he didn't count his life of any value. He was willing to lay aside comforts, friendships, and even life itself if it would honor God. His life and rights and comforts were not precious to him. Because God's glory was Paul's highest goal, he could be content in whatever way God chose to use him. God was at the center of Paul's universe.

BIG PICTURE, LITTLE DETAILS

Throughout this book we're going to be getting into the nitty-gritty of how to find true contentment in God. We'll be getting very practical, zooming in very close on different aspects of contentment. But as we study and strive for contentment, we must always keep the big picture of God's glory in mind. Our goal isn't contentment in and of itself. We're not after a mystical state of Zen. Our goal is to be content for the glory and honor of God.

So before we go any further, we need to stop and ask God to do a few things. We need to ask him to allow us to see his greatness. We can read about God's greatness in Scripture (which we should do), but we need God himself to make the words come alive in our hearts. We need God to let us see, I mean really see, his majesty, splendor, holiness, beauty, fierceness, and greatness, so much so that God captivates our hearts.

We also need to ask God to help us love his glory. In other words, we need God to give us the desire to honor him. We need God to give us a holy obsession with bringing him glory and increasing his reputation. I can't manufacture love for God on my own. I love my life too much. I count my life as too precious. I need God to help me love his honor above everything else.

The beautiful thing is that as we pursue the glory of God, we're fulfilling our life's purpose. When we seek to honor God by being content in prosperity and suffering, we're doing what we were made to do. We're glorifying God.

At the end of my life, I want to know that I fulfilled my purpose. Don't you?

STOP—THINK—DO

1. What is one situation in which you regularly find yourself acting or thinking as if you were the center of the universe?

2. Read Isaiah 6:1–7. What do these verses tell you about God? What do these verses tell you about yourself?

3. What is the appropriate response to the greatness, majesty, and glory of God?

4. What does it mean that you were created for God's glory?

5. Do you find it difficult to embrace the truth that God can do with you as he pleases? Before moving on to the next chapter, ask God to increase your love for his glory to the point where you willingly embrace his plan for your life.

3

SO WHAT AM I, A MONK?

I could never be a monk. For starters, I don't like wearing robes. I feel very insecure and unmanly when I wear a robe. Yes, I realize that wearing a robe can be very masculine and that many monks could probably beat me to a whimpering pulp in a street fight. But it doesn't matter.

A second reason I couldn't be a monk is that oftentimes they try to stifle their desires. Saint Benedict, one of the more famous monks in church history, laid out the following rules for monks entering his monastery:

- A monk could not own anything beyond what was given to him by the monastery, because property was at the root of much evil.
- Monks were to be in the habit of silence.
- Only sick monks were allowed to eat meat. Healthy monks were to abstain from all forms of meat.
- Monks were to be occupied in labor or sacred reading at all times, because idleness was the enemy of the soul.[1]

Apparently Saint Benedict was concerned about evil desires lurking in the hearts of his monks. And so, in an effort to wean his disciples from love of the world, he instituted his rules. A monk had to be content with simple monastic life.

But was Saint Benedict right? Is it only possible to obtain contentment by suppressing our desires? Do I need to become a silent vegan hobo workaholic to be truly content?

Even some of the great Puritan writers taught that contentment was learned by suppressing our desires. Jeremiah Burroughs said that a person becomes content "not so much by adding to what he would have . . . but rather by subtracting from his desires, so as to make his desires and circumstances even and equal."[2]

Or perhaps a contented person is someone who lacks ambition. Is the twenty-seven-year-old blogger/hardcore video gamer who lives in his mom's basement and seems quite happy with his life a model of contentment?

Fortunately, the answer to all of these questions is no. The Bible doesn't teach ambitionless asceticism. Content people are not desireless, emotionless Dr. Spock clones who sleep on stone floors and fake the flu so they can eat meat. Rather, Scripture speaks of a God whose presence is joy itself (Ps. 16:11), who meets all our needs (Phil. 4:19), who doesn't withhold any good thing from those who walk uprightly (Ps. 84:11), and who is the author of every good gift (Jas. 1:17). The full spectrum of emotions can be found in Scripture. The psalmist cried to God "out of the depths" (Ps. 130:1), and Habakkuk resolved to "take joy in the God of my salvation" (Hab. 3:18). Paul commands us to laugh and cheer with those who are happy and to cry with those who are broken (Rom. 12:15). This isn't the language of the stone-faced stoic. God created us to be people with desires.

But don't misunderstand. God doesn't exist to meet your every desire. He doesn't promise you health, wealth, and an attractive spouse. He doesn't guarantee three kids, a minivan, and a white picket fence. But he does promise to satisfy you, and there's a massive difference.

So what exactly is contentment? Let me provide a short definition that I hope is helpful.

Contentment is a disposition of the heart that freely and joyfully submits to God's will, whatever that will may be.[3]

Let's break it down.

CONTENTMENT IS A DISPOSITION OF THE HEART . . .

Contentment is first and foremost a matter of the heart. It's possible to deny yourself every worldly pleasure and still be discontent. I imagine that Saint Benedict encountered many discontent monks who were absolutely dying for a piece of bacon. Self-denial doesn't automatically lead to contentment. In fact, self-denial can cause us to miss opportunities to enjoy wonderful gifts from God. Steak is a gift from God. Coffee is a drink that is 95 percent heavenly. When I eat a medium-rare steak and give thanks to God for the happiness that is occurring in my mouth, I honor God. Self-denial does not equal contentment.

On the flip side, it's possible to have everything this world has to offer and still be furiously discontent. King Solomon's life was a constant pleasure cruise. He really did have everything this world could offer—money, women, power, luxury, and all the alcohol he could drink. Yet after a life of hedonistic exploits, Solomon made the following observation:

> Then I considered all that my hands had done and the toil I had expended in doing it, and behold, all was vanity and a striving after wind, and there was nothing to be gained under the sun. (Eccl. 2:11)

Solomon lived life to the hilt. He would have been *TIME* Magazine's "Person of the Year" and would have had his own cable channel. Yet in the end he still came up disappointed. Having it all doesn't equal contentment.

True biblical contentment isn't tethered to circumstances either. In Philippians 4:11 Paul says, "I have learned in *whatever situation I am* to be content." Stop and grapple with that one for a moment. When was the last time you had a *really* bad day? On your commute home from work that day, could you say, "I am really content right now"? The person who is truly content in God doesn't ride the ever-changing wave of life's circumstances.

Further, biblical contentment isn't tied to possessions. The sweaty family of six jammed into a two-bedroom shanty can be more content than the husband and wife who share a beachfront condo. In 2 Corinthians 8:1–2 Paul speaks of the Macedonians, who displayed the otherworldly combination of "extreme poverty" and "abundance of joy." These dirt-poor people, who make us look like kings by comparison, plundered their meager bank accounts for the sake of Christ. In the midst of extreme poverty, they "overflowed in a wealth of generosity" (2 Cor. 8:2). This kind of reckless generosity is possible only if contentment is not tied to possessions.

Rather, contentment is inward, untouchable by circumstances, out of the reach of trouble. It can't be stolen away by sickness or poverty, can't be ruined by the loss of a job or house or spouse. Biblical contentment is not rooted in circumstances but in the infinitely stronger foundation of God himself.

When Jonathan Edwards was fired by his church, the church he had faithfully pastored for many years, he responded in an astonishing manner. He didn't lash out at the church, didn't write an op-ed piece in the local paper, didn't start throwing out names like "narrow-minded pagans." The following observation was made of Edwards after he had been removed from his position:

> That faithful witness [Edwards] received the shock, unshaken. I never saw the least symptoms of displeasure in his countenance the whole week, but he appeared like a man of God, whose happiness was out of the reach of his enemies and whose treasure was not only a future but a present good, overbalancing all imaginable ills of life, even to the astonishment of many who could not be at rest without his dismission [i.e., dismissal].[4]

Jonathan Edwards had a contented heart that put his joy "out of the reach of his enemies." His contentment wasn't rooted in his job. His identity wasn't wrapped up in his career success. He was a man who found his treasure in God. Contentment is a disposition of the heart.

. . . THAT FREELY AND JOYFULLY SUBMITS TO GOD'S WILL . . .

Confession: I hate dentists. Well, I don't really hate dentists. I'm sure that most dentists are very nice people who just happen to have a strange obsession with teeth. I just hate what dentists do. They stick enormous needles—the kind that are used to sedate elephants and bison—into my mouth and tell me that I'm going to feel "a little pinch." They burrow into my teeth with their screaming drill from Hades. And they always ask trick questions like, "Do you get much pain in this tooth?" I'm never sure of the right answer. Should I be feeling pain? I don't know. Maybe since I'm not feeling pain, that means the tooth needs to be ripped out. Or maybe it's a good sign that I'm not feeling pain. What do I say? Regardless of my answer, I'm going to end up with a bloody, gaping hole in my mouth where a tooth used to be. I just know it.

Dentist appointments are a part of life that I tolerate. I know dentists are good for me, but I really don't like going to the dentist.

Often we treat God like some sort of divine dentist. We know, at least in theory, that he is good and that all he does is good. We know from Romans 8:28 that God works all things for the good of those who love him. But when life starts to get rough, we adopt a "grin and bear it" attitude. We know that somehow God will work everything for good, but in the meantime we're going to climb into our bunker and prepare for whatever bombs God is going to drop. This is not biblical, God-honoring contentment.

A truly contented man *freely* and *joyfully* submits to the will of God for his life. He doesn't kick and scream against the will of God. He doesn't murmur and complain about his season or circumstances of life and doesn't grumble about the things he doesn't have. A contented man isn't jealous when he sees others prospering, because he knows that God is always good to him. The contented man knows that it doesn't honor God to only *tolerate* singleness or sickness or broken dreams. Contentment freely and joyfully submits to God's will.

... WHATEVER THAT WILL MAY BE

Here's where things get difficult. I have no problem joyfully submitting to God's will when God's will involves any of the following:

- Large sums of cash, preferably in small, unmarked bills
- Unfailing health
- Regular vacations to any of the following locations: the Swiss Alps, the Bahamas, or London
- Peace, rest, and familial bliss
- A lifetime supply of darkly roasted, exotic coffee beans

But let's add a few more bullets to the above list. What if God's will involves having a tight budget? Or an engagement that suddenly ends? Or dreams for ministry that never materialize? Or a nonstop migraine headache that lasts for months, or even years? Contentment suddenly becomes much more difficult.

However, true contentment joyfully embraces both prosperity and pain as from the hand of God. Thomas Watson said:

> Whatever our condition is, God, the great Umpire of the world, has decreed that condition for us, and by his providence has ordered all the things that go along with it. Let a Christian often think to himself, "Who has placed me here, whether I am in a higher sphere or in a lower? Not chance or fortune, as the totally blind heathens imagined; no, it is the wise God who has, by his providence, fixed me in this orb."[5]

Our current condition, season, and circumstances have all been ordained by God, "the great Umpire of the world." We don't experience a breeze or backache that hasn't first been ordained by God for our good and his glory. In light of this, we must learn to be content in God's will, whatever that will may be. We must learn to sing with the classic hymn:

> *Whate'er my God ordains is right:*
> *Here shall my stand be taken;*
> *Though sorrow, need, or death be mine,*
> *Yet I am not forsaken.*
> *My Father's care is around me there;*
> *He holds me that I shall not fall,*
> *And so to Him I leave it all.*[6]

THE ROAD FORWARD

Do you feel overwhelmed? Out of your league? Unsure of the way forward? I do, and so should you. But if you know Christ, you should be full of hope. God desires that you would be content in Jesus Christ. And if you're not a Christian, thanks for reading this far, and please keep reading. There's much hope for you as well.

STOP—THINK—DO

1. Have you ever thought about contentment only in terms of self-denial? Is this a biblical view of contentment?

2. What is the difference between contentment that is a disposition of the heart and contentment that is tied to circumstances or possessions?

3. Do you ever think of God as a "divine dentist"? What does it look like to freely and cheerfully submit to God's will?

4. Write down one area of God's will for your life that you're having difficulty accepting. Begin praying that God would help you to joyfully embrace his will, even in this area. Share this area with others, and ask them to pray for you as well.

4

I WORSHIP MY TELEVISION

I don't like motivational sports slogans. They don't work. The slogans are usually something like "Pain is weakness leaving the body" or "We eat pain, and our opponents, for breakfast" and are accompanied by a dramatic photo of a bald eagle spitting lightning or a fist holding a large mallet. For some odd reason the combination of Mr. T lingo and Yellowstone National Park fails to inspire me to do anything. I prefer slogans like "No pain, no pain" or "Victory without discomfort," accompanied by a picture of a cheeseburger or television remote.

But my slogans don't sell T-shirts. And as much as I don't like them, there actually is some truth to the cheesy sports slogans. It's an unfortunate fact of life that most healing comes only after a significant amount of pain.

When my brother was in the eighth grade, he had his nose broken by an escaped baseball. Before the nose could heal properly, the doctors had to re-break it.

My friend Dan (names changed to protect the weak) snapped his Achilles tendon while playing basketball. He had to go to physical therapy for months afterward, and in order to strengthen the tendon, the therapist would put Dan's foot in positions that made him whimper and scream like a woman in labor (don't tell him I said that).

My friend Tim had his toenail surgically removed. Three times. In case you're wondering, having your toenail removed hurts. A lot. But it had to be done. The nail kept growing into the actual toe, causing the toe to become infected. The first two times the doctor removed the nail, it grew back, like some sort of invincible demon toenail. Finally, after removing the nail for a third time, it didn't grow back.

This is the part of the book where we re-break your nose, twist your foot, and rip your toenail out. This is where things get uncomfortable.

The truth is, biblical contentment can't be learned unless something else is unlearned. Contentment can't be put on without first ripping something else out. The only way to grow in contentment is to undergo the process of identifying and destroying the idols in our lives. This always hurts, but the results are wonderful.

WORSHIP MALFUNCTION

The world would have us believe that our discontentment is a circumstances problem. Given the right set of circumstances, people could be happy everywhere and all the time. And these perennially happy people actually do exist. In beer commercials. Every such commercial seems to feature a group of twenty-somethings sitting around a campfire, tossing their heads back in unrestrained laughter, and knocking back a few cold ones. These folks obviously don't have a care in the world, and if you drank lite beer on a regular basis you wouldn't either. Or so the commercials would have us believe.

But the beer commercials are a pack of barley-smelling liars. Our problem isn't a circumstances problem—it's a worship problem.

You and I are all worshipers. Everyone is a worshiper. Worship is wired into our DNA. It's what God created us to do. In Isaiah 43:6–7 we read, "I will say to the north, Give up, and to the south, Do not withhold; bring my sons from afar and my daughters from the end of the earth, everyone who is called by my name, whom I created for my glory, whom I formed and made." God put you and me on Planet Earth so that we would worship him and give him glory. That is the fundamental reason that we exist. We exist to worship. Jesus said that the greatest commandment is to "love the Lord your God with all your heart and with all your soul and with all your mind" (Matt. 22:37). Worship isn't limited to singing praise choruses on Sunday morning. Worship is loving God with all your heart, soul, mind, and strength all the time.

Unfortunately, we regularly experience severe worship malfunctions. Like a sneaky, cheating husband, we start giving our love to something other than God. Something or someone other than God mounts the throne of our hearts. Like the boy in English 101 whom you're crazy about. Or the 52-inch flat-screen television that you so desperately "need" and have meticulously researched on seven different Internet forums, including one site called "Flat Screen Ninja." Or having a toddler who takes regular naps. Or having teenagers who finally respect their father the way he deserves.

What was once a good thing that we desired becomes something we *must* have. Our affections sink their barbed fangs into it and refuse to let go. You need to be married—*now*. All your friends are married, and you're still living at home, in the same room, sleeping on Star Wars sheets. Happiness is utterly impossible until you see your bride walking down the aisle. God still has a piece of your heart, but that's all he's getting. That joy that you once found in God? Forget it. That sweet peace that came from following the Lord? That's for another time. Right now you have your heart set on finding a babe. You're no longer worshiping God—you're worshiping marriage.

Discontentment is the result of misplaced worship. It's the result of giving our heart to someone or something that should never have it. When we stake our happiness on anything other than God, we're going to be miserable. Why? Because we were made to worship God and find all our joy in him. Creation worships God (Ps. 19). The angels worship God (Isa. 6). When we worship something other than God, we're out of sync with the universe.

The Bible has a name for being out of sync with the universe. It's called idolatry. We don't use the word *idolatry* much today, except when quoting obscure lines from *Indiana Jones and the Raiders of the*

Lost Ark. But idol worship is everywhere. Do you see Mr. Pinstripe Suit going into the office every Saturday morning? He worships his job. Or Mr. Heavy Machinery Operator with the bags under his eyes? He comes home from work, collapses on the couch, and drinks a case of beer. Every night. He worships alcohol and relaxation. Do you see the pastor who savors every "what a wonderful sermon, pastor!" and is crushed by criticism? He worships the applause of people.

Idolatry is loving anything more than God. Sometimes the thing we love is wicked, like pornography or drunkenness. Most of the time the thing we love is good, like sleep or work or intimacy with our spouse. The problem is when we love a good thing too much, when we love it more than God. Tim Keller says, "If anything becomes more fundamental than God to your happiness, meaning in life, and identity, then it is an idol."[1]

Idolatry is wicked. It is an exchange of the all-satisfying God for a person, job, boat, or promotion. It is loving the creation more than the Creator, even though the Creator is infinitely more beautiful, lovely, and worthy of affection. It's as if we have a baseball-sized diamond in one hand and a mud-encrusted rock in the other, and we are forced to choose between the two. We spend several minutes studying both the diamond and the rock, holding each up to the light for closer examination. Then, shockingly, we toss the diamond aside. Idolatry is tossing aside God for a mud-spattered rock. This is infinitely belittling and insulting to God, as if something created could bring us more joy than the Creator of joy. It's a loud statement to all the world that God can't satisfy us and that we need something else.

In Jeremiah 2:12–13 (NIV) God makes the following indictment of Israel: "'Be appalled at this, O heavens, and shudder with great horror,' declares the LORD. 'My people have committed two sins: They have forsaken me, the spring of living water, and have dug their own cisterns, broken cisterns that cannot hold water.'" Idolatry is choosing muddy, briny, gag-inducing water over the fountain of living water. Idolatry is insanity.

Idolatry is also subtle. It often takes the form of a good desire, like excelling on the job, and then spirals out of control. An idol can be a good thing that we want too much, a good thing that takes the place of the greatest thing. Idol worshipers prostrate themselves before relaxation or good grades or pastoral compliments instead of God. I've been an idolater many times. I think you have too.

YOU MIGHT BE AN IDOLATER IF . . .

How can we tell if we love something too much? I love drinking coffee. Coffee is a gift from God to be enjoyed. It defibrillates my body into working properly each morning. My workday orbits around coffee breaks. Sometimes I daydream about the coffee I'm going to drink after dinner. Sometimes I dream about brownies too. Big, fat, chocolate brownies that are still slightly warm. Coffee plus brownies almost equals heaven. Not really, but you know what I mean.

Do I love coffee too much? Am I a coffee idolater? How can I know if I love coffee or brownies or work or children or anything too much? Here are several symptoms of idolatry.

You're crushed when you don't get what you want.

It's the end of the year and you have a bonus coming your way. For the past three months you've been mapping out various destinations for this bonus. A trip to Europe is one possibility. You've been wanting to take your wife to Paris for ten years, and you'll finally have the cash to make it happen. A second possibility is the screened-in back porch that you started last summer but didn't have the money to finish. The transmission of your car has been making odd moaning noises lately, and you may need to set aside money for repairs. And you still owe money on college loans for your kids. You want this bonus. Correction: You need this bonus.

Your boss calls you into his office and tells you to sit down. You expect him to say something about an outstanding year and a well-deserved reward, but something is terribly wrong. Strange, almost unintelligible words are coming from his mouth. He mentions an unexpected downturn and something about fiscal loss. He feels badly about it, but there's nothing he can do. You're fortunate to have a job, he says.

You mumble your understanding and then stumble out of his office. You stagger over to the watercooler and toss back a couple of shots, trying to steady your nerves. How can this be happening? The trip to Europe, the back porch, the transmission—all down the tubes. Shot.

For the next hour you sit at your desk and weep. Not on the outside, because you're a man and that would be weird, but on the inside. You're crushed. And angry. You're ticked off at your boss, who happens to drive a very nice car that doesn't have a moaning transmission. And you're mad at God. God knew you needed this bonus, and he didn't deliver. You know that something is wrong with your attitude, but at this point you don't give a rip. Life is so unfair.

You stake your happiness on getting what you want.

If one more person asks you to be a bridesmaid, you're going to slap her in the mouth. No, first you're going to give her a flying roundhouse kick to the stomach, then you'll slap her.

Three of your best friends have gotten married in the past six months. Each of them found a godly, attractive husband who, for the most part, was normal. You, on the other hand, can't even get a date. Well, you went out with one guy, but it was hardly a date. He talked about role-playing video games the entire time. And he had a really pasty complexion.

And it doesn't help that all the ladies in your church are having babies at a staggering rate.

You're not happy. And you probably won't be happy until you get married. Singleness is becoming a prison that you don't think you'll ever escape.

You just want to be married and have a family. Is there anything so wrong with that? Doesn't God want you to be happy? Doesn't the

Bible say something about a man leaving his parents and clinging to his wife? Last time you checked no one was clinging to you.

Your pastor keeps telling you that you should find your joy in God. Well, thank you very much, Mr. Married Pastor. Why don't you stay single this long and see if you can find your joy in God?

You grumble and complain when you don't have what you want.

Every time you look in the mirror, you grimace. You hate the way you look. You don't like the shape of your face or the proportions of your body. You wish you had a cleaner complexion and that you could do something better with your hair. Makeup doesn't do much for you. Clothes don't fit you right.

It seems like everyone around you is a beautiful person. Your friends are beautiful and attract the attention of all the guys. Pictures of beautiful men and women are splashed across magazine covers. You watch movies full of beautiful people. Even your mom is beautiful.

But not you. You got stuck with dumpy, frumpy looks that can't be fixed. And you're angry at God for giving you the short end of the stick. Looking into the mirror sends you into a tailspin of grumbling and self-pity.

You demand what you want.

Your life is hell. At least it seems that way. For the past three years you've experienced debilitating back pain. When you wake up in the morning, your back is on fire. It feels as if someone is ramming a hot knife into the lower part of your spine. Your wife has to help you get out of bed.

Pain permeates your day, invading every quiet moment. Your kids are grown and out of the house, and your wife goes to work every day. But you can't work anymore. You can barely move. Most of every day is spent lying on the couch, alone with your thoughts and the knife in your back.

You don't smile or laugh much anymore. There's no reason to. You hate your life. For two years you pleaded with God to remove the knife. Your pastors prayed, your children prayed, your grandchildren prayed. But the knife is still there. In the last year the pain has gotten worse, as if God is pushing the knife deeper.

Your prayers have taken on a different flavor in the past year. They have an edge to them, a bite. Once you pleaded with God; now you demand from him. God *must* take away this pain. After all you've done for him—teaching Sunday school, leading the choir, working in soup kitchens—the least he could do is give you some relief. You deserve it.

IDOL DESTRUCTION

In each of these scenarios, something other than God is being worshiped. An end-of-year bonus, marriage, good looks, or relief from back pain is taking the place of God and is stealing the affections that belong to God alone. A good thing has become a supreme thing. Tim Keller says, "we know a good thing has become a counterfeit god when its demands on you exceed proper boundaries. . . . An idolatrous attachment can lead you to break any promise, rationalize any indiscretion, or betray any other allegiance, in order to hold on to it. It may drive you to violate all good and proper boundaries. To practice idolatry is to be a slave."[2] The result of idol worship is always discontentment.

Idols are terrible masters. They demand our love, thoughts, affections, time, dreams, and desires. But they never satisfy, never deliver as promised. Idols always leave us in a state of dizzy discontentment.

In 1 John 5:21 we read, "Little children, keep yourselves from idols." Most of us don't do a jig of excitement when we read those words. Frankly, we've gotten a bit attached to our idols. We make sure they're well fed and get plenty of attention. The thought of giving up our pet idol isn't so appealing. We may not be able to have what we want, but at least we can dream, and that gives us some pleasure.

But playing with idols is like playing with boa constrictors. The longer an idol is left unchecked, the stronger its grip on our heart becomes. The idol crushes our heart until our love for God is almost extinguished. Idolatrous desires must be destroyed.

But how do you destroy an idol? Should you stop wanting to get married altogether? Should you toss all hopes of an end-of-year bonus out the door? No.

The solution is to *put off* idolatrous desires. In Ephesians 4:22 we are commanded to "put off your old self, which belongs to your former manner of life and is corrupt through deceitful desires." The old self represents the way we lived before we came to know Christ. Before we knew Christ we worshiped everything but God. We loved sex, money, movies, jobs, and politics more than Jesus. We were idolaters. But now that we are in Christ we must put off idolatry. It belongs to our former way of life and is totally incompatible with our new life in Christ. Now Christ demands our supreme affection, and everything else is a distant second. Jesus is very jealous. Nothing is allowed to compete with him for our love.

We put off idolatrous desires by the power of the Holy Spirit. Romans 8:13 says, "For if you live according to the flesh you will die, but if by the Spirit you put to death the deeds of the body, you will live." Idols can only be destroyed by the supernatural power of the Holy Spirit. We need the Spirit to help us identify our idols. We need the Spirit to give us a holy hatred and distaste for our idols. We need the Holy Spirit to give us a deep love for God that drives out all lesser loves. We need the Spirit to give us power over our idolatrous desires. When we become aware of an idol lurking in the shadows of our heart, we need to immediately ask the Holy Spirit for fresh power, and then we need to take action.

We take action by repenting of idols and turning away from them. To repent is to change both your *thinking* and your *behavior*. Repenting of idol worship takes different forms depending on the idol. If your idol is pornography, repentance looks like asking Jesus to forgive you for loving sex more than him. It means getting down on your knees every morning and asking God to deliver you from sexual slavery. It means having hard-hearted resolve not to fill your eyes with putrid images. It means thinking biblically about sex and lust by informing your mind with Scriptures such as Job 31:1, which reads, "I made a covenant with my eyes not to look lustfully at a girl" (NIV). It means obliterating every shred of pornography you own and asking others to help you stop worshipping sex. It might mean turning off your computer. Or destroying it. To repent of pornography is to make *every* effort to be pure.

If your idol is having children, repentance looks different. Children are a good thing, gifts from God. Repentance doesn't mean that you stop *desiring* children; it means that you stop *demanding* children from God. It means that you ask God to forgive you for loving a gift (a child) more than the Giver himself. It means that your prayers for children start to sound different. Instead of coming to God with your demands, like a divine hostage negotiator, you come with your humble requests. Instead of lacing your prayers with phrases like "I really need," you say, "I desire, but you know what I really need."

Contentment and idolatry don't mix well. Putting off idolatrous desires is the first step toward contentment. It's impossible to be content in God and worship something other than God at the same time. It just can't happen. And so the first step in finding joy is to kill the things that are killing you. It's never easy and is usually excruciating. But the sweet fruit of contentment can only blossom after you've ripped out the weeds.

STOP—THINK—DO

1. What does it mean that discontentment is the result of misplaced worship?

2. Why is idolatry so wicked? Do you take idolatry as seriously as God does?

3. What is the difference between rightly enjoying something as a gift from God and worshiping something as an idol?

4. Do you currently see any symptoms of idolatry in your life? Write these down. Share them with others. Ask God to help you clearly identify any idols in your life.

5. What practical steps do you need to take to destroy the idol(s) identified in question 4?

5

THE KING'S MADNESS

We walked into Starbucks. I ordered coffee with a splash of cream. Sol ordered a massive latte. I offered to buy Sol's drink, but he waved me off.

"Don't worry about it," he said. "I'm loaded." He flashed me a grin and pulled out a wallet that was literally overflowing with hundred-dollar bills. He carefully extracted one and then handed it to the barista (technical name meaning "one who pours coffee"), who then counted out $95 in change. Sol tossed the change in the tip jar. I choked on my coffee.

"You just gave the cashi . . . barista a $95 tip!"

Sol looked at me and shrugged. "He needs it more than I do." Sol was right. The barista had that gaunt, impoverished, almost hobo look that said, "I'm an artist." Sol, on the other hand, looked like a man who could afford to give away a few dollars. He wore a suit that probably cost more than my college education. His shoes had that expensive, foreign, bowling shoe look, and a platinum Rolex encircled his wrist. This was a guy who didn't buy from the dollar menu.

We walked over to a corner table and sat down. For a few moments we sipped in silence, and then I spoke up. "So what's up, man? It seems like something is on your mind."

Sol pondered his latte for a moment and then looked at me and said, "I'm not happy. Not at all." I was baffled.

"What do you mean you're not happy? Look at you," I said, gesturing toward his posh suit. "You're richer than I'll ever be. You're handing out cash like it's bubble gum. What is it that you want? A relationship?"

He rolled his eyes. "No, I don't want a relationship. I've done the whole relationship thing. I've been with *so* many girls. If I see a girl I want, I go after her. I've never had a girl turn me down. I've done enough relationships to know that they're not going to make me happy."

"So what then? Are you unhappy with your job?"

He gave a short laugh. "Does it look like I need career advancement? I've done more in my days than a normal person could do in ten lifetimes. I've been at the very top, the guy who signs all the checks, the guy with the corner office on the top floor."

"You're confusing me, Sol. You say you're unhappy. What is it that you want?"

"That's just it. I don't know. I've bought everything a person can buy. I could buy this store right now if I wanted to. I've done the whole education thing. I'm smarter than everyone I know, and everyone you know. I've built houses for myself and had servants waiting on me hand and foot. I've acquired more money than a person could ever possibly spend." At this point Sol was starting to get worked up.

"Sol, you need to relax. Laugh a little."

"I've tried!" he shot back. "I've gotten so drunk that a lecture on dung beetles should be funny. But I don't laugh."

"Sol, I'm sorry. I didn't realize that you were so upset." Sol swallowed the remnants of his latte. He stood up and brushed the invisible crumbs from his suit.

"It's vanity," he said. "All of it is vanity." He then strode out the door toward his cherry-red Porsche with the custom plate that said KNG SLMN.

VANITY, ALL VANITY

Okay, so I never actually met with King Solomon in Starbucks. The flux capacitor[1] on my Delorian blew out, and I wasn't able to make our meeting. But if I had, I imagine that our conversation would have been similar to the one I recounted.

Solomon was a man who had it all. Literally. He was the wisest, most intelligent man of his day, and people flocked to sit at his feet and listen to him speak. He was a dual-threat songwriter and proverb speaker. He spent thirteen years and an exorbitant amount of money building his house.

Everything Solomon did was larger than life. He consecrated the Temple by slaughtering 22,000 oxen and 120,000 sheep. In one year he stockpiled approximately 675,000 pounds of gold. Solomon had so much gold that he only drank from cups made of pure gold—silver just wasn't good enough. As if all that wasn't enough, he had 700 wives and 300 concubines. If you were to combine Albert Einstein, John Lennon, Donald Trump, Billy Graham, the President of the United States, and Bill Gates, you would have a person who still couldn't hold a candle to King Solomon.

Solomon had the resources to do whatever he wanted, which is exactly what he did. He gorged himself on pleasure and filled himself with wine. He poured himself into great architectural projects and bought hordes of slaves. He surrounded himself with singers and entertainers. He hoarded gold like a man preparing for the Apocalypse. He was a famous man, an adored man, a man sought after by others. In his autobiography Solomon makes the following statement about himself: "And whatever my eyes desired I did not keep from them. I kept my heart from no pleasure, for my heart found pleasure in all my toil, and this was my reward for all my toil" (Eccl. 2:10). This is a man who had everything that is supposed to make a person happy. He had money, sex, power, fame, a big house, and entertainment. He was a test case for human happiness. If the things of this world could satisfy, then Solomon should have been the happiest man to have ever lived. And yet, after standing at the pinnacle of life and surveying all that he had accomplished and accumulated, he came to one conclusion: "All is vanity" (Eccl. 1:2; repeated in 1:14; 2:17; 3:19; 12:8).

Solomon spent his life pursuing one pleasure after another, always searching but never finding, always looking but never discovering. What was it that drove him to such unsatisfying extremes?

In reality, we're not that different from Solomon. We have our vision of what would make us happy, of what would finally give us satisfaction. And so we pursue our dreams. We pour our energy and emotions and money into making our dreams a reality. If we're feeling really spiritual, we pray about these dreams. We pray that God would give us that one thing that would finally make our world right.

And you know what? Sometimes dreams come true. We get married, have children, land the new job, buy the new house. But we're not cured of our madness. One dream replaces another, and the circle of discontentment starts all over again.

What is it that drives us into discontented madness? The problem is that an all-out, no-holds-barred war is taking place within us. This war is between our flesh and the Holy Spirit. When the Bible uses the word *flesh*, it's often talking about our sinful nature. For example, Romans 13:14 says, "put on the Lord Jesus Christ, and make no provision for the flesh, to gratify its desires." For Christians, the enslaving power of sin has been broken, but the presence of sin remains. Our hearts, which were once under the rule of sin and Satan, are now a hotly contested battleground. God is on a mission to search out and destroy every remaining pocket of sin in us, and he *will* accomplish his mission. As we work with God in the process of sanctification, sin will be eradicated from our lives. "Victory over Sin Day" will come, either on the day we die or on the day Christ returns. But sin won't go quietly. It's entrenched and barricaded in the catacombs of our hearts. It's not about to give up its precious ground, and it will return fire. We are at war.

Like any enemy, sin has intricate battle plans, and one of its main strategies is deceit. Hebrews 3:13 says, "But exhort one another every day, as long as it is called 'today,' that none of you may be hardened *by the deceitfulness of sin.*" Sin is an expert in propaganda. It skillfully crafts lies and half-truths. My heart is trying to deceive me into believing lies, and your heart is doing the same.

Discontentment starts when we believe sinful lies—lies about God, lies about ourselves, lies about the world, and lies about others. If we're going to defeat the sin of discontentment, we need to be able to spot its lies. We need to be able to recognize propaganda. Pay attention to the following information. You'll need it for your battle plan.

LIE: GOD IS WITHHOLDING FROM ME

The universe was thrown into chaos when a man and a woman believed a lie. Adam and Eve lived in a place called Eden. Sometimes we think of Eden as something out of a Thomas Kinkade painting. A quaint place, bathed in a warm light, populated by fruit trees, fuzzy animals, and perhaps a stone bridge with a small elf sitting underneath it. A nice picture, but not somewhere we would want to live.

But nothing could be further from the truth. Eden was paradise in every sense of the word. Adam and Eve lived in perfect harmony with one another, with creation, and most importantly, with God. Because God is so generous, he told them that they could eat from every tree in the garden except one. He could have given them tasteless gruel to eat; instead he gave them a buffet.

Everything was perfect until the day that Satan invaded the garden in the form of a serpent. He came alongside Eve and said to her, "You will not surely die [when you eat the fruit]. For God knows that when you eat of it your eyes will be opened, and you will be like God, knowing good and evil" (Gen. 3:4–5).

Satan didn't mess around. He didn't try to persuade Eve that eating the fruit was worth the consequences. Instead he tried to assassinate God's character. He told Eve that God was holding out on her. In essence he said, "If God were really good and really loved you, he'd let you eat from that tree." Satan persuaded Eve that God wasn't treating her well.

Eve believed the lie and ate from the tree, and the rest is history. Sin came crashing into the world. Death took up residence among us. Murder, lying, slander, and discontentment became regular occurrences. All because Eve believed Satan's lie that God was holding out on her.

Satan ensnares us with the same lie today. We want something that is good, like ministry success, obedient children, or a relaxing life. But sometimes our dreams never materialize. Because God is infinitely wise and deeply cares for us, he only gives us what's good for us. And so we find ourselves being passed over for the promotion yet again, wondering when our day is going to come. In those moments we are particularly vulnerable to believing the lie that God is being cheap. Questions and accusations flit about our minds.

"Why won't God let me move up in my job? I've prayed and prayed and prayed for this. Doesn't he want me to be happy? He could give me what I want in a second. Maybe he doesn't love me. Maybe he's not so good after all."

The truth is, God will never withhold from us. The greatest, irrefutable proof of God's generosity is Calvary. Look at the beloved Son, ridiculed by the masses, beaten beyond recognition, hanging upon a cross, slowly suffocating, dying for sinners like you and me. God gave up what was most precious to him so that he could save sinners who hated him. If God was willing to do that, won't he also give us every good thing that we need? In Romans 8:32 Paul puts it this way: "He who did not spare his own Son but gave him up for us all, how will he not also with him graciously give us all things?"

Puritan pastor John Flavel says:

> Surely if he [God] would not spare his own Son one stroke, one
> tear, one groan, one sigh, one circumstance of misery, it can never
> be imagined that ever he should, after this, deny or withhold from
> his people, for whose sakes all this was suffered, any mercies, any
> comforts, any privilege, spiritual or temporal, which is good for
> them.[2]

If we don't have something we desire, it's not because God is
withholding good from us. God didn't spare his Son one stroke of
misery. He won't withhold any good thing from us.

LIE: GOD OWES ME

You've given up a lot for God. Once a month, for the past twenty
years, you've taught in children's ministry. You've organized food
drives and counseled young married couples who are struggling.
You haven't missed a tithe in a decade, except for that one Sunday
when you forgot to bring your checkbook and felt so guilty afterward. You're certainly not perfect, but you've put in a lot of years
for God. Surely after all these years of faithful service, God owes you
something.

Or does he? In Luke 17:10 Jesus said, "So you also, when you
have done all that you were commanded, say, 'We are unworthy servants; we have only done what was our duty.'" I have a friend who
regularly does open-air preaching at a local university. I respect him
for doing it. He gets mocked by students who are walking by, and
people don't pay much attention. To be honest, the thought of doing
that kind of evangelism scares me. And so when I see him, I thank
him for boldly proclaiming the gospel. Every time I thank him he
just says, "I'm an unworthy servant doing my duty."

I used to think that his response was kind of weird. I would
think, "Come on, man, loosen up. I'm trying to encourage you here."
But now I understand that he gets what Jesus meant. God doesn't
owe us anything. He is the Creator; I am his creation, and I owe him

everything. He puts breath into my lungs. He makes my heart beat. He doesn't owe me—I owe him. If I were to obey him flawlessly for my entire life, I would only be giving God what I owe him. All my service in children's ministry, all my prayer and Bible reading, all the times I've served my wife? I owe that to God as his servant. The time I've given up to help those who are struggling? That was my duty. I can't record my hours on a time sheet and then present them to God for reimbursement.

Can you imagine what would happen if a soldier walked into a barracks after serving on guard duty and said, "Excuse me, who is the commanding officer here? I just pulled twenty-four hours of guard duty, and I am gassed. I mean, I can barely keep my eyes open. So if I could get a bed made up for me and a glass of warm milk and possibly some slippers, that would be great. I've worked hard, and I deserve some rest." That soldier would immediately be reprimanded by his sergeant and given a year's worth of latrine duty. The Army doesn't owe its soldiers, and God doesn't owe us. Does our obedience to God put the Almighty in debt to us? Not at all. That's a lie from our discontented hearts.

But here's where things start to become slightly baffling. Though God owes us nothing, he rewards us for our service to him. In Matthew 6:3–4 Jesus said, "But when you give to the needy, do not let your left hand know what your right hand is doing, so that your giving may be in secret. And your Father who sees in secret will reward you." Something isn't right here. Why would God reward us for giving money to the poor? All the money we have was given to us by God in the first place. If he tells us to give to the poor, we obey, no questions asked, no reward expected.

But God's generosity always obliterates our expectations. Because God is so generous, large-hearted, and full of love toward us, he rewards our obedience to him. He blesses us for doing the things we're supposed to do anyway.

The discontented man complains because he isn't getting what

God "owes" him. The contented man is astonished that God would bless him for doing his duty.

LIE: IF I GET IT, I'LL BE HAPPY

All of us want it—that one thing that we're convinced will make us happy. We lie in bed at night and fantasize about it. It noses its way into our daydreams. We journal about it, pray about it, wish for it. Sometimes we budget for it. Sometimes we despair of ever getting it.

Most of the time it's a really good thing we want. And it's not wrong to want these things. It's a lie, however, to believe that getting the thing we want will truly satisfy us.

The world is full of good things, wonderful things, all made by a generous and good God. Deep friendships are wonderful. A day to ourselves is refreshing. Good health is a blessing. But God has designed these gifts to be windows through which we see him. The gifts are meant to point us to the Giver, not to be an end in and of themselves. And so God has made us in such a way that we *can't* be satisfied in anything other than himself. In his famous book *The Confessions*, Augustine said of God, "you have made us for yourself, and our heart is restless until it rests in you."[3] In Psalm 73:25 Asaph put it this way: "Whom have I in heaven but you? And there is nothing on earth that I desire besides you."

But Satan and sin work together to deceive us. They don't want us to be happy in God. They want us to frantically search for happiness in everything but God. So they whisper lies to us. They tell us that all our restlessness will be solved by a satisfying job or an easier marriage or friends who really understand us, that happiness lies just around the corner, that our discontentment is the result of not having what we want.

But that simply isn't true. We *won't* be fully satisfied when we get what we want. Because God loves us and wants us to find our satisfaction in him, he won't allow us to be satisfied. To believe that we'll finally be happy when we get what we want is a lie.

LIE: I KNOW WHAT'S BEST FOR ME

Some people are freakishly good planners. You know the type. Or maybe you are the type. Your calendar is permanently fused to your hand. You hyperventilate at the thought of making a to-do list. Sometimes you write things on a list that you've already done just so you can cross them off. Most people plan in terms of days, but not you. You have the next six months strategically mapped out, complete with bar graphs, cost/benefit analyses, and color-coded charts. And truth be told, all of us have some amount of this in us. We all have a vision of what our future is going to look like. In five years we would like to end up at a particular place with a particular person and a particular set of circumstances. Planning is good.

But things start to misfire when we think that we know what's best for us or that our vision of the future is the best possible outcome for our life. Because the truth is, we don't know what's best for us.

In Psalm 23:2–3 David says of the Lord, "He makes me lie down in green pastures. He leads me beside still waters. He restores my soul. He leads me in paths of righteousness for his name's sake." Notice that David doesn't say, "I plot the best course for my life. I am the captain of my ship. I will go wherever my heart desires." David realizes that God is his shepherd, his captain, his leader. God will lead him to places of rest. God will restore his soul. God will lead him in righteousness.

We're convinced that a particular thing will bring peace, order, and restoration to our souls. We look around, and we see other people who have what we want, and they look so happy. They skip down the street holding the hands of their little children. They gaze into the eyes of their lovers. They smile as they mow the lawn of their new five-bedroom, four-bath, three-car-garage house. Meanwhile, our lives seem so whacked out and dysfunctional.

But we really don't know what's best for our souls. If God allowed us to follow our own plans, we wouldn't end up on paths of righteousness that lead to still waters. We would end up in empty, barren wastelands of sin and destruction. God is the one who restores our soul. Sometimes he restores us by giving us what we desire, and sometimes he restores us by withholding it. In either case we can be assured that God knows the best path for us and that he'll lead us on that path.

LEARNING TO SPOT THE LIES

When I was a young teenager, I operated under the assumption that I was 95 percent omniscient. I knew what was best for me. I knew what I wanted. I knew what would make me happy. If my parents got in my way, I threw the teenager's version of a temper tantrum, complete with rolling eyes and long, drawn-out, "give me an Oscar for 'Best Dramatic Performance'" sighs.

When I was thirteen years old, I wanted to go hunting with some buddies. I, an immature kid with no hunting experience, wanted to take a loaded firearm into the woods and shoot at things.

My parents realized that this scenario could have some potential problems, like me dying, and vetoed the idea, which made me really angry. I had staked my happiness on hunting. All my friends hunted. They were tough and would tell stories about killing a gobbler at first light or taking down a buck from one hundred yards. I, on the other hand, was a dork. My stories involved beating particularly hard levels in video games. When I was told that I wouldn't be allowed to hunt with my friends, I was unhappy.

But now that I'm older and have at least a little more wisdom, I can see that my parents were right. I had believed that getting what I wanted would make me happy, which was a lie.

Today the scenarios are a little different. I don't want to hunt (although I could if I wanted to), but there are other things that I'm convinced will make me happy. So I'm trying to learn to spot the lies. I really want to be content. I don't want to end up possessed by King Solomon's madness.

STOP—THINK—DO

1. If Solomon, who had everything, was discontented, what should that tell us about ourselves?

2. What does it mean that sin is deceitful? Do you think of sin as being deceitful?

3. Have you ever thought that God was withholding something from you? How can you be sure that God will never withhold from you?

4. Have you ever felt that getting a particular thing would satisfy you? What is one Scripture that shines light on this lie?

5. Spend some time reading and thinking about Psalm 23. How does this portion of Scripture encourage you in your pursuit of contentment?

6

BLOODY CONTENTMENT

Had I lived in ancient Israel, I would have been stoned. Not in the "Hey, man, pass me another doobie" way but in the "People are throwing large stones at my head" way. Because the penalty for idolatry was serious. Death by stoning to be precise. In Deuteronomy 17:3, 5 we read:

> . . . [if anyone] has gone and served other gods and worshiped them, or the sun or the moon or any of the host of heaven, which I have forbidden . . . then you shall bring out to your gates that man or woman who has done this evil thing, and you shall stone that man or woman to death with stones.

God would not tolerate idolatry among his people. Israelites who worshiped other gods weren't given a second chance. They weren't given a pat on the back and told, "It's okay, we all worship false gods from time to time. Just make sure you tell your accountability partner tomorrow." Instead they were dragged out of the city and pelted with rocks until they collapsed in a bleeding heap of death. God wanted nothing to do with idolaters.

This raises a difficult question. How can you and I have a relationship with this idolatry-hating God? I plead guilty to the charge of idol worship. I've bowed before the idols of respect, relaxation, money, and vacation. I've loved ease and food and peace and quiet more than God himself. And I suspect that you have too.

So why are you and I still alive? Why haven't we been dragged into a deserted parking lot and executed by a firing squad? Every one of us certainly deserves it. We've all insulted God by pawning off his glory for created things. How can I, as a pastor, tell people that God will accept them, and how can I promise people that God will help them stop being idol worshipers?

THE GREAT EXCHANGE

Forgiveness of sins and power to change is possible only because of an exchange far greater than our idolatrous exchange of God's glory for created things. This exchange is a three-way transaction between God the Father, God the Son, and humble sinners who throw themselves on the mercy of God.

The first part of the exchange took place two thousand years ago when God the Son, infinite and eternal, wrapped himself in a fragile, human body. A human body that felt tired, got headaches, needed food and sleep, and had callused feet. The One who spoke each star into existence suddenly needed to rest.

The Universe Maker spent thirty-some years walking the earth, and his life pulsed with goodness. The sick were made well, the haunted were set free, mangled hands were straightened, and dead legs were made to dance. The poor and dirty found someone who would touch them, and the wicked found someone who would save them.

Sinless purity marked everything the Savior did. He never cussed after slamming a hammer onto his thumb, never stole a lustful glance, never muttered in discontentment. There wasn't a fleck of idolatry within his heart. He truly did love God with all his heart, soul, mind, and strength, and he never exchanged the glory of God for created things. He was "one who in every respect has been tempted as we are, yet without sin" (Heb. 4:15). The Savior was the only person in the history of mankind who did not deserve death by stoning.

And yet, in what would seem to be the greatest injustice ever perpetrated, the Savior, the World Maker, God Incarnate, was murdered. He was arrested by a mob of religious leaders who were jealous of God in the flesh, was tried by a governor who didn't have the courage to declare God innocent, was beaten and mocked by soldiers who had the audacity to spit in the face of God, and then was put to death in a manner usually reserved for the worst criminals. His arms and legs were stretched to the point of dislocation and then pierced by spikes. Jesus was crucified.

But in the midst of such horrors, a great exchange was taking place. At the cross, Jesus fell under the terrible, crushing hammer of God's wrath. He was punished for sins. Not for his own sins, for he had no sins to punish, but for the sins of every person who would turn to God for salvation. As noonday darkness fell upon Calvary, the wrath of God fell upon Jesus, enveloping him, crushing him, torturing him. Several thousand years prior, the prophet Isaiah had peered into the future and uttered the following words about Jesus:

> But he was wounded for our transgressions; he was crushed for our iniquities; upon him was the chastisement that brought us peace, and with his stripes we are healed. (Isa. 53:5)

The Father heaped the idolatry of millions upon Jesus and then punished Jesus as if he was the idol worshiper. It was as if Jesus was the pornography worshiper, job worshiper, and vacation worshiper.

Have you ever seen something so disturbing and revolting that you couldn't bear to watch? On the cross, Jesus was worse. He became so spiritually grotesque in the Father's eyes that the Father would no longer look upon him. And so Jesus cried out, "My God, my God, why have you forsaken me?" (Matt. 27:46). The Son of God exchanged his purity for our wickedness.

Steve Estes and Joni Eareckson Tada capture this truth powerfully, imagining the Father speaking to the Son:

Son of Man! Why have you behaved so? You have cheated, lusted, stolen, gossiped—murdered, envied, hated, lied. You have cursed, robbed, overspent, overeaten—fornicated, disobeyed, embezzled, and blasphemed. Oh, the duties you have shirked, the children you have abandoned! Who has ever so ignored the poor, so played the coward, so belittled my name? Have you ever held your razor tongue? What a self-righteous, pitiful drunk—you, who molest young boys, peddle killer drugs, travel in cliques, and mock your parents. Who gave you the boldness to rig elections, foment revolutions, torture animals, and worship demons? Does the list never end? Splitting families, raping virgins, acting smugly, playing the pimp—buying politicians, practicing extortion, filming pornography, accepting bribes. You have burned down buildings, perfected terrorist tactics, founded false religions, traded in slaves, relishing each morsel and bragging about it all. I hate, I loathe these things in you! Disgust for everything about you consumes me! Can you not feel my wrath?[1]

There are no words to describe the horror that Jesus endured on the cross. Those who are in hell right now are getting a faint glimpse of it, but even their sufferings are insignificant compared to the suffering of the Son of God. They are being punished for their sins only. Jesus was punished for the sins of millions. Jesus was wrapped in the filth of millions of wicked acts, and God treated him as if he had committed every one of those acts.

The second exchange takes place the moment a sinner cries out to God for salvation. In that moment God forgives every sin he or she has ever committed and credits the sinless life of Jesus to him or her. The sinner's discontented idolatry is exchanged for the Savior's perfection. God now treats the sinner as though that individual is righteous, sinless, and perfect. His sins are totally removed, and he is fully righteous in God's sight. The alcoholic who spent his days blowing out his mind with whiskey is now clothed in robes of righteousness. The business executive who sacrificed his marriage on the altar of the paycheck is now washed clean. The pastor's kid who reeked of self-righteousness now has true righteousness. Second Corinthians 5:21 describes this glorious exchange when it says, "For our sake he [God] made him [Jesus] to be sin who knew no sin, so that in him we might become the righteousness of God." Instead of being condemned to hell, the sinner is promised eternal joy in the presence of God. Heaven is the final destination of those who trade their wickedness for Christ's righteousness.

This is how idol worshipers can be brought into fellowship with God, and how a holy, righteous God can forgive those who have exchanged his glory for created things. Christ became our filth; we become his righteousness. He was crushed for our sins; we are wrapped in his righteousness. He was forsaken by God; we're welcomed into the presence of God. Our wicked exchange is swallowed up in the greatness of the divine exchange.

Now let's stop and ponder. If this were all we received in salvation, wouldn't it be enough to fuel an eternity of contentment? We deserve hell, but we receive heaven. We run toward wrath but instead are pulled into the arms of forgiveness. We curse God's name and in return are washed in the blood of Christ. This is the greatest exchange in the history of the universe. Could we ask for anything more?

But there is more.

NEW HEARTS

If the gospel brought forgiveness of sins but didn't give power over sins, it would seem like a cheap trick. After all, what good would it be if our idolatry was forgiven but we still lusted after every shiny thing that crossed our path? What good would it be if our sins were forgiven but we couldn't stop worshiping idols? Thankfully, the gospel doesn't leave us floundering in our sin but always delivers a payload of heart-changing power. True salvation is always followed by a dramatic heart change.

Ephesians 2:4–5 describes this heart change in terms of death and life:

> But God, being rich in mercy, because of the great love with which he loved us, even when we were dead in our trespasses, made us alive together with Christ.

Prior to salvation we were spiritually dead, glassy-eyed, idol-loving God-haters. We had no love for God and no power to obey him. We were hopelessly in love with the sin that was killing us, and we couldn't have stopped our idol worship if we tried. We were like a woman who regularly gets busted up by her angry husband but refuses to leave.

But because God is bursting with mercy and overflowing with love, he made us alive. Our spiritually dead hearts suddenly pulsed with life, and new desires blossomed in our heart—desires to please God, love God, and kill sin. The power of sin was broken, and the chains that tethered us to our idols were snapped. Our idols no longer rule us. A decisive, mighty victory has been won, and now we're living in the wonderful fallout of that victory.

Do you remember when your spiritual heart started beating? Do you remember when Jesus first set you free from the power of sin? Do you remember the gleeful "I can't believe this is real" sense of joy you felt when sin's miserable power was broken?

The goodness of the gospel almost seems unreal, unfathomable, unbelievable! It seems too good to be true, too wonderful to be real. There has to be a catch or a bait and switch—nothing can be this good, and nothing can be this free.

But it is, and there's even more.

GOSPEL BLESSINGS

The death and resurrection of Christ kicks down the door to the warehouse of God's blessings. Those who trust in Christ are given access to an astonishing collection of riches—far more than we would dare ask or imagine. Let me give you just a taste, a spoonful from the gourmet buffet.

Fellowship with God

In the gospel we have full, free, open access to God. This isn't "come once a year, kill a lamb, and hope you don't die" access to God. We don't need to whip ourselves into a twirling religious frenzy or to light sticks of incense. There's no need to walk ten miles with broken glass in our shoes or wash ourselves clean in a sacred river. We can come into the presence of God at all times and at all places.

This is the greatest benefit of the gospel. Forgiveness of sins, a new heart, and eternal life are only a means to this magnificent end. Jesus Christ ushers us into the presence of God, and it's in the presence of God that we find our soul's deepest satisfaction. Psalm 16:11 says, "You make known to me the path of life; in your presence there is fullness of joy; at your right hand are pleasures forevermore." A speedboat, job promotion, or beautiful, loving spouse who likes long walks on the beach can't bring fullness of joy. Eternal pleasures can't be purchased with a platinum credit card. Full, overflowing, eternal joy and pleasure are found only in the presence of God, and in the gospel we have access to his joyful presence.

John Piper, who always puts it much better than me, says:

> What makes all the events of Good Friday and Easter and all the promises they secure good news is that they lead us to God. . . . And when we get there, it is God himself who will satisfy our souls forever.[2]

If we want contentment we need to spend time, much time, lingering in the presence of God. We need to go to the place where contentment is found, to regularly drink from the fountain of joy. We need to let our eyes pore over the pages of sacred Scripture and to listen closely as God speaks to our hearts. We need to commune with God by praying to him and by fellowshipping with the people of God. If we're not consistently spending time in the presence of God, we won't be content. Period.

So often we spend countless hours killing ourselves to obtain what we think will satisfy us. We go into the office on weekends. We wade through dozens of house listings. We take relational compatibility tests based on forty-two separate categories that are guaranteed to match us with that perfect someone. None of these things are inherently wrong, but they can't satisfy either. Trying to satisfy ourselves with these things is like downing a pint of saltwater when we're thirsty. It's insane. And there's something so much better. A contented man says to God, "For a day in your courts is better than a thousand elsewhere" (Ps. 84:10).

Every day we'll be tempted to be discontent. Even if you hit the lottery tomorrow and are able to heat your house by burning bales of hundred-dollar bills, you'll still be discontent. But through the gospel we have the unshakable, always available, always satisfying source of contentment—God himself. The gospel of Christ makes it possible for us to dwell with and be truly satisfied in God.[3]

Children of God

As if things weren't already baffling, through the gospel we become children of God. Prior to conversion we are divine terrorists. We spit in God's face, kick dirt on his commands, and do everything in our power to sabotage his plans. It would be incredible if God did nothing more than forgive us and allow us to be lowly servants in his kingdom. But he does far more than that. He lifts us out of the gutter scum, cleans our filth, wraps us in clean robes of righteousness, and then embraces us as children. Rebels are adopted as sons and daughters. You can almost see John's open-mouthed wonder as he declares, "See what kind of love the Father has given to us, that we should be called children of God; and so we are" (1 John 3:1).

I have a little girl who is two years old, and the affection I feel for her is almost overwhelming at times. Everything she does makes me grin. She pushes Winnie the Pooh around in a stroller, and I grin. She points and giggles at low-flying airplanes, and I grin. She passes gas in that innocent "did I do that?" sort of way, and I . . . you get the point. I love this little girl with all my heart. And my love doesn't hold a candle to God's love for us.

In Zephaniah 3:17 God says, "The LORD your God is in your midst, a mighty one who will save; he will rejoice over you with gladness; he will quiet you by his love; he will exult over you with loud singing." Our lives have a glorious soundtrack. God loves us so much that he exults over us with loud singing. He is so glad to have us as his children that he is singing over us.

Every morning we wake up as children of the King. We're adopted, loved, treasured, and blessed. No trial, circumstance, need, pain, or heartbreak can ever separate us from the intense love and compassion of our Father. God's love pursues us relentlessly and zealously. Paul describes this hurricane of love when he says in Romans 8:38–39, "For I am sure that neither death nor life, nor angels nor rulers, nor things present nor things to come, nor powers, nor height nor depth, nor anything else in all creation, will be able to separate us from the love of God in Christ Jesus our Lord." God's love for us is invincible, unbreakable, and unshakable. The legions of hell can't defeat it. There is no future we can imagine apart from it. Even death itself buckles before the almighty love of our Father.

You may not have an earthly father, but you have a heavenly one who loves you far more than any earthly father. You may not have a husband to shelter you, but you have a heavenly Father who shelters and protects you (Ps. 36:7). You may not have everything that you want, but your Father promises that he will meet all your needs (Matt. 6:26).

This truth is life-giving for the discontented heart. Do you want to be more content? Spend a day or a week or a month or a decade marveling and wondering at your divine adoption. You are a child of God. The Creator of the universe really is your Father, and he loves you with an intense, fatherly affection. He cares for you with the heart of a father. He hears your requests with the heart of a father. He watches over you with the diligent eye of a father. Reflect on and rejoice in every difference between your former state (rebel) and your current state (son or daughter of God). Thank God for adopting you instead of sending you to hell. Thank God for calling you "child" instead of "enemy." Fill your mind with the massive truth of adoption. You'll soon find yourself dizzy with joy and gratefulness.

Eternal Life

Death is not doing well in the popularity polls these days. Everyone is trying to escape the clutches of death. Every morning millions of women lather up with age-defying, skin-exfoliating cream, determined to force every wrinkle out of their faces. Men dab Rogaine on their expanding bald spots and brush in beard dye to give themselves that rugged Burt Reynolds "why, yes, that is my convertible" look. We live in a culture that is absolutely terrified about death, and for good reason. For those who don't know Christ, death is a launching pad into eternal torment. The terrible, burning, furious wrath of God awaits those who die apart from Christ. There is no resting in peace, no going to a better place. Enemies of God are doomed to an eternity in hell.

But glorious things await those who have taken shelter in Christ. In John 4:14 Jesus promised, "whoever drinks of the water that I will give him will never be thirsty again. The water that I will give him will become in him a spring of water welling up to eternal life." We have the prospect of eternal, joyful, ever-increasing, God-saturated life ahead of us. Christ defanged death, stealing its terrifying power. Death ushers us into the immediate presence of Christ, and in his presence is "fullness of joy" and "pleasures forevermore" (Ps.

16:11). Most of the world trembles at the thought of death, but not Christians. We know that "to die is gain" (Phil. 1:21).

Our future with Christ transforms how we view the present. Our joy isn't chained to our relational status, television size, or health because we know that this life is a passing mist that will soon be burned away by the glory of heaven. We can patiently endure heartaches and headaches because we know that glory is coming. Thomas Watson said, "Whatever change or trouble a child of God meets with, it is all the hell he shall have."[4] We may have trouble now, but it is all the trouble we will ever have. We may have sorrow now, but it is all the sorrow we will ever have. We may be under pressure now, but it is all the pressure we will ever have. Eternal life is ours, and the prospect of eternal joy fuels our present joy.

A MOUNTAIN AND A MOLEHILL

Now let us stop and stare and stammer at the great mountain of gospel blessings that lies before us. Let's take a nice, long, gaping look. We don't deserve such blessings, and we shouldn't have them. But we do have them! Far more than we would ever dare ask for or imagine.

Now let's pick our slack jaws up off the dusty floor and look at the things that are causing us to be discontent. The job promotion that we so desperately want. The husband who will finally fulfill all our desires for intimacy. The house, the education, the girlfriend, the fishing trip. Come on, pile them all up.

Do some comparisons between the two piles. One is a glorious heap of blessings designed to bring us satisfaction and joy from now until eternity. The other is a dingy pile of thrift store goods that will never satisfy the longings of our hearts. All the things that we so desperately want can't compare to the wonder of knowing Jesus Christ. He's the treasure of the universe, and because of the gospel, we have him. And he has us.

In Philippians 3:8–9 Paul said, "I have suffered the loss of all things and count them as rubbish, in order that I may gain Christ and be found in him." The word "rubbish" carries the meaning of garbage, refuse, and even animal dung. Paul considered all the treasures of this world to be putrid animal dung compared to the glory of gaining Christ. If you had a steaming pile of dog feces in one hand and a diamond in the other, which would you choose? Because of the gospel, we get to keep the diamond.

Does the gospel cause us to pulse with gratefulness? Are we able to chuckle in a light, condescending manner at all the treasures of the world and then say, "I have Christ—I don't need them"? Do we ever stop and happily scream at the heavens, "Why, O God, would you be so kind to a sinner like me?"

Thomas Watson says:

> Are you not heir to all the promises? Do you not have a foretaste of heaven? When you let go of your natural life, are you not sure of eternal life? Has not God given you the earnest and first fruits of glory? Is not this enough to spur the heart to contentment?[5]

The gospel of Christ is the fountainhead of contentment. In the gospel we have access to infinite blessings. But if we don't drink often we will always be thirsty. The moment I feel the saltwater-like thirst of discontentment, I need to plunge again into the gospel. I need to stop and stare and wonder and laugh at the goodness of God in the gospel. I need to spend time working on my gospel math, calculating the infinite distance between what I deserve and what I've received. To marvel that a prodigal like me could be embraced by the Universe Maker as a son. To imagine the gutter of misery I would be lying in if Christ had not rescued me. If I want to overcome discontentment, I need to spend time wallowing in the gospel.

CUTTING THE NERVE OF COMPLAINING

Do you see how the gospel should obliterate complaining? Complaining is almost always rooted in a faulty sense of rights and privileges. Each of us has a lengthy list of things that we think we deserve. When life starts to short-circuit and we don't get what we "deserve," we start complaining. We imagine ourselves as the injured party who has every right to complain. We don't think we should have to endure hardship, and so we grumble about our stressful job, or our rickety back, or our disrespectful children.

But the gospel makes it very clear that the only thing we truly deserve is hell. God created us, and therefore he owns us. As created, dependent beings, we owe him complete, unwavering allegiance and obedience. Yet all of us have rebelled against our Creator. We have shaken our puny fists at God and raised our insignificant voices to curse his name. We've told God that we can run our own lives, thank you very much, and that he can stick to his side of the tracks. We've gorged on his blessings, like sunshine, food, and vacation, but wanted nothing to do with the Giver himself. We've told our Maker to stay away.

God owes us nothing except justice. The fires of hell would be the right destination for ungrateful, arrogant rebels like us. We've been disobedient, rebellious, hard-hearted people. We don't deserve relaxation or a nice house or hot showers or a monthly paycheck. What we *deserve* is hell.

But the beauty of the gospel is that we get what we *don't* deserve. Instead of justice, we receive mercy; instead of wrath, grace. God has forgiven us, adopted us, clothed us in righteousness, given us the Holy Spirit, and promised to hunt us down with mercy (Ps. 23:6). Every morning we awake to the song of new mercies. On our worst days we're always doing infinitely better than we deserve. We may not get what we desire, but we have immeasurably more than we deserve.

In his book *The Rare Jewel of Christian Contentment*, Jeremiah Burroughs makes the following statement:

> So I may say to a Christian: Are you the King's son, the son, the daughter of the King of Heaven, and yet so disquieted and troubled, and vexed at every little thing that happens? As if a King's son were to cry out that he is undone for losing a toy; what an unworthy thing would this be! So do you: you cry out as if you were undone and yet are a King's son, you who stand in relation to God, as if either he had not wisdom, or power, or mercy enough to provide for you.[6]

When we complain, we're loudly saying that the blessings of the gospel aren't enough. We're saying that the death of Christ isn't enough. We're saying that eternal fellowship with God, purchased at great cost to God, isn't enough to satisfy our souls. We're saying that forgiveness of sins and peace with God is nice, but not that nice. We're saying that God "[has] not wisdom, or power, or mercy enough" to provide for us. We're saying that God himself, who is the very definition of goodness, isn't good enough. We would like a little something more, if you don't mind. God plus [insert desire of choice] should do the trick. When we complain, we accuse God of being stingy, of not giving us enough.

Do you see the utter sinfulness of complaining? It tramples the gospel in the mud and paints God as a cosmic Scrooge. Even though God gave up what was most precious to him to bring us to himself, it's not enough. Even though God proved his generosity with blood, we don't believe him. God has emptied his pockets for us, and yet we complain.

The only way to cut the nerve of complaining is to regularly and actively remember and savor and apply the gospel. Complaining doesn't fare well in the soil of thankfulness, and the gospel should always propel us to deep gratitude. When the lie of "I'm not getting what I deserve" starts to simmer within us, let's remember the hell we deserve and the heaven we've received.

ASTONISHED AT THE DIFFERENCE

The book *The Valley of Vision*, a book of Puritan prayers, contains the following words:

> *O Lord, I am astonished at the difference*
> *between my receivings and my deservings,*
> *between the state I am now in and my past gracelessness,*
> *between the heaven I am bound for and the hell I merit. . . .*
> *O that such a crown should fit the head of such a sinner!*
> *such high advancement be for an unfruitful person!*
> *such joys for so vile a rebel![7]* ("The Mover")

Are we astonished at the difference between our "deservings" and "receivings," astonished to the point where gratefulness crowds out discontentment? If we're not astonished, something needs to be rearranged in our hearts. Let's ask God to astonish and baffle us afresh with the gospel so that we might find our contentment in him.

STOP—THINK—DO

1. What is the divine exchange, and why is it our only hope? How does thinking about and rejoicing in the divine exchange help us grow in contentment?

2. On the left side of a piece of paper, write down every gospel blessing that you can think of. On the right side, write down the things that are causing you to be discontent. Is there really any comparison?

3. What do you deserve? What have you received? When was the last time you thanked God for the massive difference between the two?

4. Are you more aware of the things that you don't have or of all that you have received in the gospel? How can you grow in gratefulness for the gospel?

5. Why does the gospel leave no room for complaining?

7

SOME PEOPLE HAVE TO LEARN THE HARD WAY

I'm a very needy individual. Or at least that's what the experts tell me. According to renowned psychologist Abraham Maslow's "Hierarchy of Needs," if I don't receive food, shelter, love, sex, self-esteem, self-actualization, and the NFL Sunday Ticket from DIRECTV, I'll be a very unhappy person who spends his days panhandling for change on street corners.

But Maslow was way off. I need much more than self-actualization. Let me tell you what I really need to be happy. I need to own a house that has a sprawling backyard surrounded by friendly neighbors who are fond of giving me monetary gifts and/or T-bone steaks and is located in a neighborhood that is drug-free, bully-free, and speed-walker free.[1] And I would like that house right now, if you don't mind.

I need a salary that gives me the freedom to buy whatever I want (see above reference to fantastic house) whenever I want it, which is usually right now.

I need career success, which for me means having a church that is packed to the rafters every Sunday with people who use the following words/phrases to describe me: revival, Charles Spurgeon on steroids, manna from heaven, the greatest pastor in the history of Christendom who wasn't also an apostle. Oh, and if I could get that right now that would be great.

And I really need some rest. I recently had one of those lingering colds that makes you feel ill but isn't bad enough to keep you home from work. You know the kind I'm talking about. You haul yourself into the office, only to spend most of the day clearing out your nose and feeling like garbage. Then you come home and try to sleep but can't because it feels like you're breathing through a sweaty T-shirt. I need rest.

If the apostle Paul and I happened to be best buds and were sitting in Starbucks sipping Venti cups of coffee and discussing my needs, I think he might lovingly and gently throw his coffee in my face. Not in a sinful way, but in a way that says, "I care."

Then, after mopping my Sumatra-spattered face, he would say, "Stephen, let me tell you about needs. Have you ever been beaten with sticks to the point where every movement sets your joints on fire?" I would shake my head no. Then he would trace his finger along a jagged scar running from his cheek to his eye and say, "Have you ever had an angry mob throw stones at you until you passed out?" Again, no. Then he would lift the back of his shirt just enough to let me catch a glimpse of his back, a tangled web of scar tissue. "Have you ever been whipped to the point where your back is in bloody strips?" I would meekly shake my head. Then Paul would smile at me and put his hand on my shoulder. "In each of those situations I had things that felt like needs. But in the middle of it all I learned something very important: how to be content. I haven't always been a content person. I had to *learn* it." At least, I think that's what Paul would say.

PAUL WOULD HAVE BEEN ON OPRAH

In Philippians 4:10–11 we read:

> I rejoiced in the Lord greatly that now at length you have revived your concern for me. You were indeed concerned for me, but you had no opportunity. Not that I am speaking of being in need, for I have learned in whatever situation I am to be content.

These are strange words from the apostle Paul. In all likelihood he was writing to the Philippians from Rome, where he was in prison and possibly awaiting execution.[2]

But Paul doesn't seem to be concerned for himself. He's not thrashing to get back into ministry, not cursing the prison walls that hem him in. He doesn't even see himself as being in need. Paul actually uses the word "content" to describe how he feels about his time as a prisoner. In fact, Paul says he has learned to be content in *every* situation.

Does this seem like crazy talk to anyone else? Paul, author of much of the New Testament and gospel preacher extraordinaire, is in jail. He can't do much ministry behind bars. No gospel preaching, no church planting, no satellite campuses. Paul's career seems to be at a standstill. The gospel looks like it might have stalled out. Death is standing just around the corner, leaning against the wall and pulling on a cheap cigarette. And yet you can almost see Paul smiling as he writes to the Philippians. He's content.

Do you realize the extravagance of Paul's claim? "*I have learned in whatever situation I am to be content.*" This is the kind of claim that gets you on Oprah and sells millions of books. Rich business executives hire life coaches to teach them this kind of thing. Gurus climb the Himalayas to find the inner life force that will give them this kind of contentment. I desperately want this kind of circumstance-free contentment, don't you? How did Paul arrive at such a place?

LEARNING THE HARD WAY

Paul's contentment wasn't the result of a mountaintop spiritual experience, and he didn't learn it from the pages of a best-selling book. He didn't have the demon of discontentment cast out of him. More importantly, Paul wasn't content because things were going well for him. The dice were not rolling Paul's way when he wrote to the Philippians. Paul had a contentment that transcended circumstances. If you met Paul in prison, he would have had a joyful smile on his face. If you met Paul relaxing in his home, the smile would have still been there. Paul had *learned* to be content.

This implies that Paul wasn't always a model citizen of contentment. In times past he may have stalked the confines of his prison, shooting sinister glances at the guards, kicking at the walls, and muttering complaints under his breath. He couldn't always claim to be content in every circumstance.

Over the years, however, something changed in Paul. He was transformed from discontent to content, from complaining against God to joyfully submitting to God, from raging to praising. He learned to cheerfully and humbly submit to God's will, even when that will involved prison, hunger, or stoning.

But change never takes place in a vacuum, and Paul was certainly no exception. His transformation was the result of being squeezed, shaped, and pressed by the various circumstances that God brought to him. In Philippians 4:12 Paul writes, "I know how to be brought low, and I know how to abound. In any and every circumstance, I have learned the secret of facing plenty and hunger, abundance and need."

God brought Paul low. Very low. He was stoned to a bloody pulp by an angry mob.[3] He was beaten with rods three times[4] and had his back mulched by a whip five separate times.[5] Paul was shipwrecked at least four times.[6] Did he still have scars and divots in his head from the stones? Did the repeated beatings cause him to walk with a limp? How many days did Paul lie on his stomach while his back was healing? How many nights did Paul spend in the ocean, clinging to a piece of driftwood and pleading with God to wash him up on the beach? Paul knew lowliness in a way that few of us will ever experience.

And yet it was in the midst of this lowliness that God taught Paul the secret of contentment. Paul learned to be content in suffering *only* through suffering. He learned how to be content with hunger only after feeling sick and dizzy with malnutrition. God allowed Paul to prosper so that he would learn how to enjoy abundance without clinging to it. Paul's supernatural contentment was the result of being placed in circumstances that were beyond his strength, which forced him to cry out to God for contentment. I can imagine Paul pleading with God for strength as a friend dabbed his ruined back with a damp cloth. I can see him holding his bloodied head between his hands and blessing the Lord. Paul's supernatural contentment was learned in the hills and valleys of life.

We too must *learn* the skill of divine contentment. We are by nature discontent. We're not going to wake up one morning and suddenly be possessed by an overwhelming sense that all is right in the world. Taking yoga, eating a balanced diet, and becoming one with nature won't produce contentment. Getting what we want when we want it won't bring lasting happiness. Joyful contentment is the result of hard-fought, blood-sweat-and-tears battle. God is eager for us to have the same joyful, peaceful, circumstance-free contentment that Paul had, but it's something we must learn. Charles Spurgeon says, "Now, contentment is one of the flowers of heaven, and, if we would have it, it must be cultivated. It will not grow in us by nature; it is the new nature alone that can produce it, and even then we must be especially careful and watchful that we maintain and cultivate the grace which God has sown in us."[7]

How do we see our current circumstances? Do we see them as divine training grounds, forcing us to press and strain toward the wonderful goal of contentment? How do we see our angry, disrespectful children who don't yet know the Lord? Do we see them as endless sources of frustration or as instructors from God in the school of contentment? How do we think about the limitations that God has placed upon us? In his wisdom God has given many men and women more talents and abilities than us. Do we chafe against our limitations or embrace them as means of learning contentment? Or what about our razor-thin budget that barely has room for the things we need, let alone the things we want? Every pain and every prosperity is an opportunity from God to learn the priceless art of contentment. Thomas Watson says, "If God dams up our outward comfort, it is so that the stream of our love may run faster in another way."[8]

As I write this, I'm in the process of trying to buy a house. There's just one small problem: almost all of the houses in our price range are dumps that appear to have been inhabited by sheepherding hoboes for the last ten years. And the one house that does have potential appears to be sitting in the middle of a flood zone, which could be a major problem. But in the midst of my house hunt, God is teaching me. He's teaching me to be thankful and content with the house that we rent (which is wonderful). He's teaching me to be grateful for the numerous blessings I enjoy every day, like coffee and hot showers and football and a little girl who screams "Daddy!" when I walk in the door. And he's teaching me to rest in his care for me. God is using my circumstances to teach me contentment. I couldn't learn it any other way. What circumstances is God using to teach you contentment?

GOD ISN'T YOUR FOOTBALL COACH

We won't learn contentment, however, if we treat our circumstances like high-school football camp. Football coaches are fond of screaming motivational phrases at their players like "Suck it up!" or "Fight through the pain!" or "Your mom called and she wants her dress back!" The coaches want their players to learn toughness, self-reliance, and inner strength. This may work for football, but it won't work for contentment.

It's not enough for us to just take our circumstances, like we're taking a punch in the face. We won't learn true, blessed contentment if we grit our teeth and kick our way through life. Life isn't an Iron Man competition. Instead our circumstances should drive us to God and cause us to cry out for the strength to be content.

In 2 Corinthians 12:7 Paul speaks of his thorn in the flesh, a messenger from Satan to harass him and keep him from becoming conceited over the incredible revelations he had received. We don't know exactly what this thorn was, but we know that it made Paul miserable. Three times he pleaded with God to remove the thorn. Three times he asked for peace, for relief, for rest. But God wouldn't grant Paul's request. Instead he gave Paul something better than relief: grace. God said to Paul, "My grace is sufficient for you, for my power is made perfect in weakness" (2 Cor. 12:9). Paul asked for relief, and instead he received power—power that was perfected in weakness. God gave Paul that thorn so that Paul would lean upon God for grace. The thorn stripped Paul of self-reliance and caused him to press into God. Paul's utter weakness forced him to cling to the God who gives sustaining strength. What thorn are you enduring right now? Is it pressing you into God or pushing you away from God?

Paul's experience of strength in weakness gave him a new perspective on trials. In 2 Corinthians 12:10 he says, "For the sake of Christ, then, I am content with weaknesses, insults, hardships, persecutions, and calamities. For when I am weak, then I am strong." Paul was content to be insulted. When I'm insulted, I want to go to war. Not physical war, because unless I was insulted by a six-year-old I would get my teeth busted out. I'm talking verbal warfare. I want to go on the attack against my offender. But not Paul. He was content to have his name insulted and dragged through the mud by his enemies. He was content to endure hardship and persecution. And he was content to endure calamity. Calamity? Calamities are heartbreaking. They cause us to sob and doubt and wonder what God is doing. Brain cancer is a calamity. Stillbirth is a calamity. Yet Paul was even content to endure calamity for the sake of Christ. Why? Because insults, hardships, persecutions, and calamities drove him deep into the living God, and there he found soul-sustaining grace. The unbearable weight of Paul's circumstances forced him to find strength and contentment in God. Paul could be content in all things because he went to God in all things.

When life seems unbearable we have two options. We can grumble and complain and sink into a pit of unbearable depression and discontentment; we can curse our circumstances and long for the day when we'll finally be happy. Or we can run to the God whose power is made perfect in our weakness, the God who gives contentment in the midst of calamity. In the midst of trials we never expected, God wants to give us grace that we never expected. We simply need to ask. For example:

- Lord, I don't think I can endure this migraine another day. Please sustain me! Help me not to complain. Help me bless your name. Please give me relief.
- Father, if my son is disobedient one more time, I think I'm going to scream. I desperately need contentment. Help me be patient with him.
- Oh, God, we still can't conceive a child. My heart is breaking right now, but I know that you are full of compassion. Please help me to joyfully and contentedly submit to your good will.

My dad is a wonderful example of a man who has learned contentment. For many years my mom has battled a serious, at times debilitating, illness. There have been days when it was difficult for her to get out of bed or make dinner or clean the house. Initially these were tough days for my dad. He was tempted to complain when he had to wash dishes or do laundry. He didn't want to make dinner after spending all day working. He just wanted to relax.

But I've witnessed a transformation in my dad. Instead of allowing his circumstances to rule his life, he ran to God for strength. He prayed that God would help him to be content with dishwashing and housecleaning and caring for my mom, even after an exhausting day of work. He prayed it again, and again, and again. God answered those prayers. Slowly but surely my dad learned to be content. He learned to find happiness in God right where God had him. My dad is my hero, and I want to be like him.

How do you respond when life goes from difficult to impossible? Do you wallow in discontentment and complaining, or do you run to God? Do you allow your circumstances to determine if you'll be content, or do you go to the God who gives joy that transcends circumstances? Our God gives sufficient grace to weak, easily discontented people. Lean on this grace. Cling to this grace. When life seems unlivable, find shelter in this grace. Don't try and wade through life on your own. It's suicide. Run to the God who uplifts us in our weakness.

I NEVER WAS IN PRISON

When I was twelve years old, I was in a homeschool choir. I chuckle as I write those words.[9] The words *homeschool choir* are funny in and of themselves, like mime choir or Sylvester Stallone choir. But the concept isn't as funny as the songs we sang. One year we sang the song "The Hard Way" by my all-time favorite Christian rock group, dcTalk. The song talks about people who have to learn things the hard way and to find out everything for themselves. The music video was black-and-white and was shot in a prison, giving the whole song a feeling of toughness and street cred, as if it were being sung by a hardened ex-convict.

In a key part in the song front man TobyMac goes into a rap solo, rhyming about "warning signs" and "flares in the night" and the need to stay out of trouble.

When the choir did the song, I had TobyMac's part. So imagine if you will a skinny white kid with his hair parted from the side whose greatest act of rebellion to that point had been continuing to play Nintendo when his mom asked him to let the dog out, rapping about learning the hard way. It was a sight to behold.

But let me tell you something. I rapped the pants off that song. If I had been wearing giant, multicolored pants I could have easily been mistaken for MC Hammer.

Looking back on my brief rapping career, I realize what a silly thing it was for me to sing about learning the hard way at the age of twelve. I never served time, never did drugs, never even smoked a cigarette. God saved me at a young age, sparing me from that kind of heartache.

But in a sense I could still be singing that song today. I really do have to learn the hard way when it comes to contentment. There's no shortcut, no easy way out. Contentment is learned. God is teaching me to be content in the midst of pain and prosperity, gladness and sadness. I'm not there yet, but I desperately want to learn to be content in *all* circumstances. I'm a slow learner, but I am learning.

STOP—THINK—DO

1. If contentment is something that must be learned, how do we learn it?

2. How do you view your circumstances? Do you see them as divine opportunities to grow in contentment?

3. What circumstances is God currently using to teach you contentment? How are you responding to those circumstances?

4. Why is it so crucial for us to run to God in the midst of difficult circumstances?

5. Is your natural tendency to try and push through difficult circumstances without relying on God's grace? If so, what is one way you can grow in becoming more dependent on God?

8

IN SEARCH OF THE SECRET

Selling secrets is a big business these days. For $49.99 you can learn the secret to making millions of dollars in the stock market while working from home in your flannel Star Trek pajamas. For just a few dollars a day you can learn the secret to perfect, robust health: regular colon cleansing (did I ruin the secret?). If you aren't fond of your company, you can commit industrial espionage and sell company secrets. If you happen to work for the government and also happen to hate your country, you can make millions by selling top-secret information to a foreign agent named Boris.

And let's not forget about the book/movie *The Secret*, which has turned into an international best seller. Claiming to usher in "a new era for mankind," *The Secret* "reveals the most powerful law in the universe." If you read the book, you will learn how to "transform any weakness or suffering into strength, power, perfect peace, health, and abundance." Contained within the pages of this book is the secret to "prosperity, health, relationships, and happiness."[1] I have to admit, that sounds even more appealing than colon cleansing.

The apostle Paul had a secret too, a secret that would have blown *The Secret* out of the water. It was a secret of epic proportions, the kind of secret that would have made him millions of dollars had he been selling it. Paul had learned the secret of being content in all circumstances.

In Philippians 4:11–12 Paul writes:

Not that I am speaking of being in need, for I have learned in whatever situation I am to be content. I know how to be brought low, and I know how to abound. In any and every circumstance, I have learned the secret of facing plenty and hunger, abundance and need.

The promise held forth in these sacred verses is breathtaking: contentment in any and every circumstance. Consider all that falls under the umbrella of "any and every circumstance." Sleepless nights with a restless toddler. A promotion at work. A devastated 401(k) package. Beautiful twins born without a single complication. A baby lost in the last week of the pregnancy. Getting to see your grandchildren grow up. Being diagnosed with cancer at age forty-five.

Is it really possible to be content in all the glory and pain that we encounter in life? Is true, unshakable, unbreakable contentment possible? It is if you know the secret.

PAUL'S SECRET

Paul's secret wasn't complex or mystical. It didn't involve discovering a secret herb used by Aztec Indians, or channeling the power of his inner strength, or learning to suppress all his desires. Paul didn't need a comfortable house, career success, or sexual satisfaction to find joy. He needed one thing, and one thing only: Jesus Christ.

In Philippians 4:13 Paul writes, "I can do all things *through him* who strengthens me." When I played Little League baseball I had this verse inscribed on the bill of my hat. The verse functioned as a sort of spiritual motivational speaker, reminding me that I could do all things (*I can't hear you!*), ALL THINGS, including hitting the daylights out of a baseball, through Christ who strengthened me. Some ballplayers get fired up by listening to rock music or slapping each other on the side of the head. Not me. I didn't need those gimmicks. I had Scripture on my side.

But to be honest, this verse didn't improve my skill set one bit.

When I was ten years old, I stunk. I couldn't field and was terrified of getting hit by the ball, which makes it difficult to hit. Turning eleven didn't help. It only made me more embarrassed when I struck out. When I was twelve years old I started playing really well, but that was because I started practicing. Apparently my Philippians 4:13 amulet didn't work.

I don't think, however, that God ever intended to teach us principles of athletic success through Philippians 4:13. God has something much bigger and glorious and God-glorifying in mind. He wants us to find lasting joy and contentment in Jesus Christ.

True contentment is found in a Person. It's not found in getting what we want or in having difficulty removed from our lives. Contentment isn't the result of the absence of pain or the presence of material blessing. It's found in Jesus Christ. Period. Without Christ we can never be truly content, regardless of the blessings that surround us. And with Christ we can be content in the midst of every circumstance.

IN ALL YOU DO, GO TO CHRIST

If it's true that contentment and joy are only found in Jesus, if Jesus is the cure for discontentment, then it's crucial for us to cultivate a deep relationship with Jesus. He is *the* supply of true contentment. We can't get it anywhere else. If we want to be content in all circumstances, we must draw our strength from Christ in all circumstances. We need to be continually close to Christ. There's no other alternative. Life is too bitter and difficult, and our hearts are too sinful to survive on our own.

Many people in my church are in the midst of difficult suffering. Some are coming face-to-face with the devastating effects of multiple sclerosis. Others are bearing the heartache of children who are not following the Lord. Some are under such intense financial pressure that they haven't slept well in months. How are these folks able to endure such suffering without becoming bitter toward God? Only

Jesus himself, the one who sustains and strengthens, can give true contentment in the midst of such brutal suffering.

Even if we're not facing intense trials, life is still hard. Our parents' health deteriorates, and our children suffer. We're harassed by pain in our shoulders, legs, joints, and head. We lose jobs and friends and have trouble sleeping at night. Escaping hardship is impossible. It permeates every facet of our existence.

Oddly enough, contentment in God can be just as difficult in the midst of prosperity as in the midst of troubles. Prosperity can lull us into a dull worldliness, a spiritual sleepiness that can dampen our love for Christ. We can be so comfortable in this life that we don't feel our desperate need for God, and we end up trying to find contentment in a world that will never satisfy us. Prosperity is like saltwater. It takes the initial edge off our thirst, only to leave us ravenously thirsty a few hours later.

The only way to satisfy our thirsty souls is to find our satisfaction and strength in Christ. When we're brought low by fever or singleness or infertility, Christ is the one who strengthens us. He's the one who empowers us to joyfully embrace God's will, whatever that will may be. I choose the word *joyfully* intentionally. Joyfully embracing God's will doesn't mean that we're always laughing or smiling. There's not much laughter around a death bed or in the emergency room. To joyfully embrace God's will means that during the sobs and sorrow we say to God, "I bless your name, for you are always good to me." Only supernatural power can enable a person to contentedly bless God in the midst of life's hurricanes. Jesus is the one who gives that supernatural power. He's the one who strengthens us to be content in hunger, need, lowliness, and sickness. Christ is the secret to contentment in suffering.

The prophet Habakkuk discovered the secret of contentment. In Habakkuk 3:17–18 we read:

Though the fig tree should not blossom, nor fruit be on the vines, the produce of the olive fail and the fields yield no food,

the flock be cut off from the fold and there be no herd in the
stalls, yet I will rejoice in the LORD; I will take joy in the God
of my salvation.

These are the words of a man who was determined to find his
joy in God, even when his world was collapsing. If the fig tree didn't
blossom and there was no fruit on the vine, there would be no food
to eat. If the olives failed, the fields were granite, the flocks were
decimated, and there wasn't a single ox in the barn, he and his family
would die a slow, hungry death. But even the prospect of these bleak
circumstances couldn't break Habakkuk's joy. Why? Because his joy
wasn't anchored in prosperity but in the God of his salvation.

If Habakkuk had written today he might have said something
like this:

> Though I lose my job, and my retirement package is shattered and
> my house destroyed and my health ruined, yet I will rejoice in the
> Lord; I will take joy in the God of my salvation.

How can we find joy in the midst of sorrow and contentment in
grief? By taking joy in the God of our salvation, the God who loves us
and purchased us with the blood of Jesus. By remembering that the
cross proves that God is 100 percent on our side and that if we face
any affliction, it's from the hand of our Father. We find contentment
by holding Romans 8:31–32 in a white-knuckled grip: "What then
shall we say to these things? If God is for us, who can be against us?
He who did not spare his own Son but gave him up for us all, how
will he not also with him graciously give us all things?"

Christ is also the one who empowers us to be content in abundance. There will be seasons of joyful abundance when our health
is excellent, our friendships are rich, and we experience blessing at
every turn. These things are wonderful gifts from God and should
be enjoyed with thankfulness. But they can be even more dangerous
than seasons of suffering because they tempt us to find our refuge in

things other than God. We're tempted to rest in our bank account and trust in our 401(k). When we feel discontent we can go to the mall and shell out a few bucks for a new pair of pre-ripped jeans and a few moments of happiness. We can try to bury our discontentment under a mountain of possessions.

If we're to honor God in seasons of prosperity, we must receive strength from Christ. Only supernatural power can protect us from spiritual dullness. Only Christ's strengthening power can keep us from loving the creation more than our Creator. Only Christ is able to help us find our contentment in God and not in things. Apart from Christ, our love for God will be smothered by the things of this world. Christ is the secret to contentment in prosperity.

FINDING CHRIST IN PROMISES, PRAYER, AND PEOPLE

It sounds good to talk about going deep with Christ, but what does this look like practically? What exactly must we do to draw strength from Christ? Fortunately there's nothing mystical involved. There's no need to light any candles or chant any lyrics in a monotone voice or wear a drafty robe. We meet Christ through promises, prayer, and people.

Strength in Promises

I'll admit, I'm a cynic when it comes to customer satisfaction promises made by corporations. Companies promise 100 percent customer satisfaction and then fail to deliver. The flash on my wife's digital camera recently stopped working. She sent the camera in for repairs, only to discover that it would cost $169 dollars to replace the flash. Talk about a baffling disappointment. $169 to fix the flash? Apparently it must be made of gold-encrusted diamonds.

One particular company, which I won't name but rhymes with Mal-Wart, used to promise 200 percent satisfaction on their baked goods. They were promising that their cookies could give me double total happiness. I could be wrong, but I think they were promising something that was physically impossible. The point is, businesses fail to live up to their promises.

But God never fails to deliver on his promises. In 2 Corinthians 1:20 we read, "For all the promises of God find their Yes in him [Christ]. That is why it is through him that we utter our Amen to God for his glory." The Bible is full of promises from God, and all these promises to us find their "yes" in Christ. In other words, when we are joined to Christ through the gospel, we are brought into the blessing of all God's promises. When we read the Bible and see a promise, we can say, "Yes, this does apply to me! God is making this promise to me because Christ has bought this promise for me with his blood."

In the Bible we find an endless supply of contentment-giving promises. We find verse after verse in which God has promised to strengthen us, build us, sustain us, and encourage us. In one sense the Bible is a record of what God has committed to do on behalf of his children. These promises are our life. They infuse hope into darkness and life into death. If we want to be happy, we need to sink our foundations deep into these promises. Jeremiah Burroughs says:

> There is no condition that a godly man or woman can be in, but there is some promise or other in the Scripture to help him in that condition. And that is the way of his contentment, to go to the promises, and get from the promise, that which may supply.[2]

To survey and apply all the glorious promises of God would take hundreds of books. So instead let me draw your attention to just a few massive promises. Let me whet your appetite for the promises of God.

In Philippians 4:19 we read, "And my God will supply every need of yours according to his riches in glory in Christ Jesus." Our God has promised to meet our every need. We won't have a single true need that won't be met by God. Every real need will be fully satisfied.

Because God is wise and knows that often we want things that would really be harmful, he won't give us everything we *desire*. But he will give us everything that we *need*. Can you see the generosity of God bursting from this verse? God meets our needs according to his *riches* in Christ Jesus. We don't have to pry open God's clutched, clammy fingers to persuade him to meet our needs. God isn't like a dad who looks like he's passing a kidney stone every time his kids ask him for a few dollars. He's rich, and he meets our needs out of his riches. Do we believe, I mean really believe, that God will meet our every need? He's a rich God who lavishly scatters his riches to all his children. In his book *The Art of Divine Contentment* Thomas Watson says:

> God has engaged Himself under hand and seal for our necessary provisions. If a king should say to one of his subjects, "I will take care of you . . . If you are in danger, I will secure you; if in want, I will supply you," would not that subject be content?[3]

The King has promised to care for us, provide for us, protect us, and supply us. Isn't that enough to make us content?

Romans 8:28 says, "And we know that for those who love God all things work together for good, for those who are called according to his purpose." This is an explosive, contentment-creating promise of God. Every event that occurs in our lives has been ordained by God for our good. God is moving all things—singleness, sickness, riches, poverty, children, and infertility—toward one destination: our good and his glory. God is using your constant headaches for good. He's weaving together your recent job promotion, sick daughter, and inability to fix your flooding basement into something glorious and good. There is *nothing* that can happen to us that God won't use for good. In fact, the very things that tempt us to be discontent are being used by God for our good.

We need to hold this promise close to our chests when we're feeling discontent. It should be burned into our minds and branded on our hearts so much that we instinctively turn to it in the midst of discontentment. God is working all things for our good. Good will blossom from bankruptcy. Good will spring forth from a broken friendship. Good will bloom in the desert of depression. We may not see it, and we probably don't feel it, but we must believe it and stake our very lives upon it.

The author of Hebrews writes, "Keep your life free from love of money, and be content with what you have, for he has said, 'I will never leave you nor forsake you.' So we can confidently say, 'The Lord is my helper; I will not fear; what can man do to me?'" (13:5–6). How is it possible to be free from the love of money and to be content with what we have? By remembering that we have something far greater than money: the constant presence of Jesus. We won't always have enough in the bank. Our salary may get slashed, or we may lose thousands of dollars from our retirement account. Business may get unbearably slow. But we always have Jesus. He will never leave us or forsake us.

As I write this, I'm aware that my budget is uncomfortably tight. It just happens to be one of those times when all the bills are colliding in a perfect storm and my bank account is having the life sucked out of it. A tight budget tempts me to be greedy. I want more money. I want the temporary peace of mind that a fat wad of cash gives. Hebrews 13:5–6 is a weapon to be wielded in the battle against greed. When I'm tempted to be greedy, I need to remember and rejoice in the constant presence of Jesus. Even if I were to lose all my earthly possessions, I would still have the Pearl of Great Price. I don't need to find my security in a bank account because I have the steady presence of Jesus. I can be content with what I have because I have Jesus.

In Psalm 84:11 we read, "No good thing does he withhold from those who walk uprightly." When we're discontent, we believe that God is holding back from us. If God really loved us, he would give us that thing we so desperately want—a house, a spouse, a car that doesn't start to shudder and shimmy at 60 mph. But Scripture spells it out in black and white: God won't withhold a single good thing from his children. If a thing is good for us, God will give it to us. If it's not good, he'll withhold it. And in God's kindness, he doesn't allow us to pick and choose what we would like in our lives. If we were allowed to choose what we thought was best for us, we would self-destruct. In the words of Thomas Watson, "We fancy such a condition of life good for us, whereas, if we were our own carvers, we should often cut the worst piece."[4] Thankfully, God doesn't allow us to carve out our own lives. He carves out our days, and then he fills them with goodness.

The promises of God are our weapons in the battle against discontentment. For every temptation to be discontent there's a promise of God that meets that temptation. The abundant grace of God promised in the Scriptures far exceeds any circumstance we encounter.

But if we're going to fight discontentment effectively, we need to stockpile our weapons. When temptation strikes, we need to have go-to promises to sustain and strengthen us. There should be pages in our Bible that are tattered and torn from constant use. We should have Scriptures scribbled on index cards and pasted on our bathroom wall and by the kitchen sink and on our dashboard. A soldier would never go into battle unarmed; yet so often we try to battle discontentment without any weapons. We can't expect to win the battle if we aren't stocked up on ammunition. The promises of Christ are our ammunition. Christ strengthens us through his promises.

Strength in Prayer

What's on your prayer list right now? Probably some personal spiritual needs, like patience with your maniacal children who travel about the house in destructive herds. There's probably also the spiritual needs of others, like the struggling couple in the church and your child who doesn't seem to be following the Lord. And then there are your own physical needs. You ask for some cash flow to pay the heating bill. You ask God to remove the persistent pain in your back. You regularly pray that God would give your husband a better job. When Jesus instructed us to ask for our daily bread (Matt. 6:11), he was inviting us to pray for our physical needs. It's sinful and stupid not to present our material needs to God.

But when we're discontent, our prayers for material needs/ desires can dominate everything else. We pray and pray and pray for that thing we so desperately desire. We enlist prayer partners to intercede on our behalf. We fill out prayer cards so our pastors can get in on the action. After a while our prayers start to get edgy and demanding. We no longer humbly say to God, "Your will be done." Instead we say, "Give me, give me, give me. I need. I need. You owe this to me, God!" We're no longer happy with just God. No, no. We need God plus children or a girlfriend or job security. Our desires for other things begin to choke out our love for the Lord.

How do we avoid praying demanding, worldly, discontented prayers? How do we find contentment in Christ through prayer? By asking for spiritual eyes. In Ephesians 1:18–19 Paul tells the Ephesians how he prays for them. He prays that they would have

> . . . the eyes of your hearts enlightened, that you may know what is the hope to which he has called you, what are the riches of his glorious inheritance in the saints, and what is the immeasurable greatness of his power toward us who believe, according to the working of his great might.

Paul doesn't ask God to provide the Ephesians with the best cuts of lamb or the cushiest apartments in downtown Ephesus. Instead Paul asks God to give the Ephesians spiritual sight so that they might see the riches they already have in Christ. Paul wants the Ephesians to know the hope to which they've been called, and to understand their riches in Christ, and to feel the immeasurable greatness of God's power that's at work in and toward them. Paul wants the Ephesians to glimpse and grasp and feel and be astonished at the treasures they've received in salvation. He wants them to be so gripped by what they've received that what they desire becomes dim background noise.

Have you ever seen the show *Antiques Roadshow?* Here's how it works. PBS brings together the best antiques experts in a particular city and then invites the general population to bring in their antiques to be appraised. Most people overestimate the value of their antiques and bring in junk that they found in their grandmother's attic or at a yard sale. These folks are always sorely disappointed when the experts tell them that the moldy piece of paper they're holding is just a moldy piece of paper and not an original letter written by Christopher Columbus from the New World.

But occasionally the reverse happens. Someone brings in an old, tarnished, beat-up sword that they've had hanging over their fireplace for the past twenty years. They hope that it's worth a couple hundred bucks but brought it in out of curiosity more than anything. When the expert sees the item, he starts to get excited. He points out minute details like the engraving on the handle and the faintly visible markings on the blade. He calls for backup and consults with other experts. Finally, after minutes of tense anticipation, the expert will finally say to the owner, "Do you have any idea how much this is worth?" The owner will shake his head and say, "I really have no idea. A couple hundred dollars?"

The antiques expert will then tell a fascinating story about how this particular sword belonged to General Robert E. Lee and was used at the Battle of Gettysburg to slice watermelons and is now worth approximately 2.5 million dollars. At this point the owner is usually stuttering with excitement. Suddenly the owner no longer views the sword as a rusty relic hanging over his fireplace. He has eyes to see the true value of the treasure, and he leaves with a new appreciation for what he owns.

When we feel discontent, we need to have an *Antiques Roadshow* experience. We need to ask God to open our eyes to see the incredible wealth we have in Christ and to be filled with gratefulness for all that we've received. It's not enough to know that we're rich in Christ. We need to know it and feel it and be overwhelmed that God would give such riches to such sinners. Christ strengthens us when we pray that our eyes would be opened to see the value of what we truly have.

Strength in People

We live in a culture that is bursting with individualism. From the moment we enter kindergarten we're told that we're special, unique individuals who need to find our way in the world. Professional athletes are praised for their individual achievements, and Gatorade wonders, "Is it in you?" We love the story of the self-made man who overcame poverty and a dysfunctional family to become CEO of a major corporation. We are the culture of the cowboy, the loner, the Marlboro Man, the rugged individual who conquers all obstacles and achieves his greatest dreams.

But there is no room for Marlboro men in the kingdom of Christ. In 1 Peter 2:9 we read, "But you are a chosen race, a royal priesthood, a holy nation, *a people for his own possession.*" God is creating a people for himself through the redemption of Christ. He's not creating millions of isolated, one-man armies. He's creating a people who have been bought by the blood of Christ and joined together to bring honor to God together. No solo acts allowed.

This means that our growth in contentment will only happen in connection with other Christians. We cannot grow in contentment apart from the body of Christ. It's simply not going to happen. Hebrews 3:13 says, "But exhort one another every day, as long as it is called 'today,' that none of you may be hardened by the deceitfulness of sin." Here's the frightening part: sin is deceptive. My sinful heart lies to me, promising me joy, pleasure, and contentment in things other than Jesus. My heart tells me that sexual sin will make me happy, that a new tool will make me happy, that time to myself will make me happy. Sin is deceitful, and I'm in danger of being hardened by it.

But here's the good news: I find protection from the deceitfulness of sin in the company of other believers. I need godly friends to help me see through the sinful lies of my heart to the truth of God's Word. I need friends who will turn my gaze away from my circumstances to the God who never changes. I need companions who will say, "Stephen, you're believing a lie. God is the source of true joy and satisfaction."

Commenting on Hebrews 3:13, Paul Tripp says, "The Hebrews passage clearly teaches that personal insight is the product of community. I need you in order to really see and know myself. Otherwise, I will listen to my own arguments, believe my own lies, and buy into my own delusions."[5]

Are you receiving the insight that comes from community, or are you listening to your own arguments and believing your own lies? Do you have one or two close friends who know the ways that you struggle with discontentment and who can help you in the fight? Do you bring others into your battles against discontentment, or do you try to wage war alone? Do you enlist others to pray for you, challenge you, and bring the correction of God's Word to you?

Without the insight and correction of others, we won't overcome discontentment. Because we receive the strength of Christ through other Christians, we must not fight the battle on our own.

A ROUT WITHOUT CHRIST

A battle lies before us. Will we honor God by being content in all circumstances, or will we grumble and mope and murmur? Will we fight against the discontentment in our hearts, or will we be bullied and beaten by our own desires? If the outcome of the battle hinged on our strength, all hope would be lost. But it doesn't. Christ is our strength, and in him we really can be content in all circumstances. There is enough strength, joy, and life in Christ for us to be content. We simply need to draw upon that strength.

Let these words from Charles Spurgeon encourage us in our battle:

> Take heed, however, that you get Christ's strength. You can do nothing without that. Spiritually, in the things of Christ, you are not able to accomplish even the meanest [most ordinary] thing without Him. Go not forth to your work, therefore, till you have first prayed. That effort which is begun without prayer will end without praise. That battle which commences without holy reliance upon God, shall certainly end in a terrible rout.[6]

The battle waged without reliance on Christ will be a rout. I don't want to be routed by discontentment. I want to fight it through the One who strengthens me.

STOP—THINK—DO

1. Does the prospect of contentment in every circumstance seem impossible to you? According to Philippians 4:13, what is the true secret for contentment in all circumstances?

2. What does it mean that contentment is found in a person? Are you finding your contentment in the person of Jesus Christ?

3. Do you fight against the sin of discontentment with the promises of God? What is one Scripture that can, or will, help you in your battle against discontentment?

4. When was the last time you asked God to help you see the riches you have in Christ?

5. Do you have others helping you fight against discontentment? What will the outcome be if you try to fight discontentment on your own?

9

EAT THE MEAT AND DIE

The birds lay so thick upon the ground that you couldn't see the dirt beneath them. It was an unbelievable sight, as if millions of birds had heart attacks simultaneously and instantly dropped to the ground. The sea of corpses was at least three feet deep.

Men, women, and children waded through the sea of downed birds, whooping and shouting and grinning. Some of them threw feathers in the air. Others tossed birds back and forth in a bizarre game of catch. "We have meat!" one man shouted. "Finally some variety. We've been eating the same thing month after month, but not anymore. We're going to barbeque tonight!" The people loaded up basketful after basketful of the birds. One basket, five baskets, ten baskets—it was starting to get absurd. No person could eat this much meat. Not in a day, not in a month. But it didn't matter. The people didn't want to miss out on this opportunity. They hadn't eaten meat for months, and they were going to collect as much as possible.

A caravan of people staggered back to the camp, hunched over under thousands of pounds of bird. Once they arrived at camp, they began preparing to eat. The birds were plucked and gutted. Fires crackled, and mouths watered as bird after bird was skewered and placed over the heat. Husbands smiled at their wives as they slowly rotated the birds. Children skipped around the camp singing, "Meat, meat, we want to eat." The whole atmosphere felt like a big, happy party.

Then death struck. A man's eyes rolled back into his head, and he collapsed beside his fire. A woman made a gurgling noise, like water running through a rusty pipe, and then fell to the ground. One by one the people collapsed and died, leaving their fires unattended and their meat to rot. Soon the ground wasn't covered with birds but with people.

What could cause such a plague? Was the meat poisoned? Were they ambushed by an enemy? Did they contract a violent, organ-liquefying virus? In Numbers 11:33 we discover the cause of death: "While the meat was yet between their teeth, before it was consumed, the anger of the LORD was kindled against the people, and the LORD struck down the people with a very great plague." God himself was the killer.

But what would cause God to strike down these people? They must have been engaged in a wicked pagan practice, like child sacrifice or moon worship. What wicked sin were they committing that would lead God to strike them dead? They were complaining. In Numbers 11:1 we read, "And the people complained in the hearing of the LORD about their misfortunes, and when the LORD heard it, his anger was kindled."

Complaining is one of those sins that doesn't get much airtime in our churches. We talk about big sins like lust, greed, selfishness, anger, adultery, and violence. These are the sins that populate our sermons and accountability meetings. By comparison, complaining seems pretty minor. We stand around the watercooler at work and complain about our boss. We sit in our cars with scowls on our faces and complain about the traffic. We moan about gas prices, computer meltdowns, broken radiators, and flu symptoms. Complaining is part of our life. We know it's wrong, but it doesn't seem like a big deal.

But God takes complaining very seriously. It's not a little sin in his eyes. In Bible times, people died because they complained against God. People who murmured against the Lord were playing with death. Complaining is serious business.

Complaining is like smoke. Smoke proves there's a fire somewhere, and complaining proves that discontentment is nearby. Discontentment and complaining go hand in hand. If we're going to kill discontentment, we need to kill complaining. And if we're going to kill complaining, we need to get our minds around why complaining is so wicked.

AN UNKIND MASTER

Complaining isn't just an insignificant, minor, everyday sin. It's a slap in the face of God. When we complain, we're saying that God hasn't been good to us. We're making a loud statement to ourselves and to the rest of the world that God hasn't been a good master. As we step back and survey our lives and our circumstances, we come to the following conclusion: God did something wrong. Sure, he's gotten us out of some jams. Sure, he did the whole salvation thing for us. He's thrown us a bone every now and then. And yes, he's given us a family and a house and a car and all that stuff. But overall we're not too happy with the way God has run things. If it was up to us, things would be a lot different. And so we complain.

But in reality no one has been kinder to us than God. He gave us his precious Son, the one whom he treasured, to save us. He pulled us from the filthy gutter of our sin. We insulted him, ran from him, hated him, and told him to leave us alone. He chased us, caught us, washed us, welcomed us, and made us his children. Every morning we wake up experiencing new, fresh mercy from God. Psalm 103:4 describes God as one "who crowns you with steadfast love and mercy." He's promised never to leave us or forsake us. He's working everything together for our good. He's preparing a place for us in heaven. He's coming back to claim us as his own. He'll preserve us through temptation and trial until we stand before his throne. Then he'll reward us for our weak, flawed acts of service to him, and we'll be with him forever, experiencing the joy of a new heaven and a new earth.

Complaining is blindness. Blindness to all that God has done for us. Blindness to the mercies that surround us. Blindness to the blessings that greet us with the sunrise. It's as if we're standing on top of a mountain of gold coins complaining about the quarter we lost. God has dumped many, many blessings on us, and we're whining about the one thing we don't have.

Years ago my mom and dad won a Caribbean cruise. They had a blast. Every day they lounged around the deck, basking in the sun, listening to music, and snacking on cruise food. Every night they made their way down to the gorgeous "Midnight Buffet"— gourmet food in all-you-can-eat quantities. In small-town redneck Pennsylvania we don't get these kinds of luxuries. We're pretty happy with a bag of Fritos from the local gas station. So as you can imagine, my parents were in heaven, so to speak.

By the end of the cruise, however, my dad's attitude had changed. He wasn't as dazzled by the luxuries. In fact, he even began to notice some things that he wished were different. One night at the buffet he held up a massive shrimp and said to my mom, "You know, Kristi, I think these shrimp would be better if they were a little bit smaller." Instantly my dad realized the utter absurdity of his statement. He was sitting in the lap of luxury, gorging on gourmet food, and complaining that the shrimp were too big.

How often do we lift our heads from the buffet of God's blessings only to voice a complaint? We're surrounded by mercies, enjoying more than we could have ever asked for or imagined, and we're complaining because we're stuck in traffic. Because we don't own a house. Because our coworkers mistreated us. We're saying that God hasn't been good to us, that he's not so kind after all. We're telling a lie about God. That's why complaining is so wicked.

I'm writing my own prosecution. I complain, and so often it's about the most trivial things. I just put new tires on my car three months ago, but apparently those tires were made of tofu or some other soy-based product, given how quickly they disintegrated. So

I stand at the buffet of God's blessings and complain about needing new tires. I need grace to change.

Thomas Watson says, "our base hearts are more discontented at one loss than thankful for a hundred mercies. God has plucked one branch of grapes from you, but how many precious clusters are left behind?"[1]

What are you tempted to complain about? When you start getting that generally annoyed, "I'm about to complain" feeling, take a step back, survey the blessings, and thank God for his generosity.

A HELPLESS GOD

As a good, orthodox Christian, I like to talk about God's sovereignty. This term simply means that God is in control of everything. An insect can't die apart from God letting it happen.

I passionately sing songs that affirm God's sovereignty. God is my mighty fortress, the Rock of Ages, my help in ages past. When someone is going through a tough time, I pull out my sovereignty sword of Romans 8:28 and remind them (or beat into them?) that God is working all things for good. And truth be told, the doctrine of God's sovereignty has been a shelter for me in the midst of really hard times. Oh, I know about God's sovereignty all right.

But many times there's a short circuit between my knowledge of God and the way I live. I know in my head that God is sovereign and that nothing comes into my life unless he ordains it. I drink coffee from a mug that says "TRUST." I'm usually rocking God's sovereignty.

Until my life starts to get hard. Until I get really sick. Until my dreams get put into a holding pattern. Until I don't have the success for which I was hoping. When these things happen, I want to complain.

When I complain, I'm preaching to myself and everyone else that God is helpless. I'm saying that God doesn't know what he's doing when it comes to my life, that God is a new driver behind the wheel of the universe. When I complain, I inform the world that God isn't very good at running my life. If God knew what he was doing, I wouldn't be [insert your particular struggle]. Stuck in a dead-end job with an insane boss. Battling a health disorder. Unable to find steady work that will allow me to provide for my family.

The funny thing is, God has proven again and again that he knows exactly what he's doing. He's proven it first through his Word. In Proverbs 3:5–6 we read, "Trust in the LORD with all your heart, and do not lean on your own understanding. In all your ways acknowledge him, and he will make straight your paths." God has a detailed blueprint for my life. He knows where I've come from, and he knows where I'm headed. These plans are good plans, plans for a good future, plans overflowing with hope. God's plan for me is overwhelmingly good, and He'll make it happen. Over and over God assures me through the Scriptures that this is the case.

My experience has also proven that God knows how to run my life. God has always, *always*, *ALWAYS* been faithful to me. When the budget has been tight, God has been faithful. When life has been full of stress, God has always met me and strengthened me. In the very little amount of suffering I've faced, God has upheld me. God has used all these circumstances to make me more like Jesus. And God has been faithful to you too, hasn't he?

When I complain, I'm declaring that I serve a helpless, bumbling God. That my life is out of control. That he hasn't been faithful. That he isn't using circumstances for good. I'm smearing God's character and forgetting his past faithfulness. I'm telling the world that God is a pathetic, disorganized deity who can't seem to get my life straight. I'm telling a lie about God.

PUTTING GOD ON TRIAL

Call the defendant to the stand. Do you swear to tell the truth, the whole truth, and nothing but the truth?

The accused is charged with the following crimes: dangerous neglect of family, failure to give child support, and family abandonment. This person is a deadbeat and a menace to society. He needs to be taken off the streets and locked up until he can get his act together. The name of the accused: God.

The previous scenario occurs millions of times each day. It occurs when we curse rush-hour traffic. It occurs when we complain about our house, which is so small compared to other houses. It occurs when we grumble about the government, our boss, our wife, or our lousy car that keeps making that funny whirring sound even though we've already had it in the shop three times. When we complain, we accuse God. We drag God to the witness stand and demand that he give an account for his actions. We want to know why he allowed this particular circumstance to occur when he had the power to make things different. Complaining turns us into prosecuting attorneys.

The people of Israel also leveled accusations against God. The Lord had orchestrated a jailbreak of epic proportions for the Israelites, using blood, hail, frogs, flies, locusts, boils, darkness, gnats, disease, and even death to break the Egyptian hold over Israel. He led them into the desert, directly into the heart of the Red Sea. The Egyptian army pursued them and was obliterated when the Lord set the walls of water back in place. For forty years the Lord provided them with bread and water in the desert, which isn't a place known for producing bumper crops of bread or water. Finally God led them to the edge of Canaan, the land he had promised to give Israel.

Israel sent spies ahead to scout the land and bring back a report to the people, but the report wasn't good news. Canaan was populated by giant, hulking, God-hating people. These weren't the kind of folks you would invite over for a game of Hearts and a slice of manna on a Saturday night. These were the kind of people who would bust your brains out. For fun.

Israel was terrified. And angry. They said, "Because the LORD hated us he has brought us out of the land of Egypt, to give us into the hand of the Amorites, to destroy us" (Deut. 1:27). The Israelites accused God of hating them. God had done everything in his power to bless them, and the Israelites accused God of hatred. They complained against God. They moaned and wept. God had only shown them kindness, and they responded with accusation.

The consequences of their false accusations? They were kept out of the Promised Land. It's a serious thing to accuse God of being a deadbeat deity.

When we complain, we're accusing God of hating us. Of not caring for us. Of not meeting our needs and not being a good Father. We're accusing God of deliberate neglect. He has the power to make our world right. To heal us. To bring us a spouse. To provide a job that will cover the heating bill. If he doesn't do these things, then he must be an awful, unloving God. So says the complainer.

These are horrible accusations. No one has been kinder to us than God. No one has done more to prove his love. He killed his Son to prove that he is 100 percent for us. He adopted us. He calls us his children, and we call him Father. What more do we want from him?

Complaining turns us into blasphemers.

A JOYLESS LIFE

My first boss was not a nice guy. His name was Don, and he had been the sole proprietor of the local hardware store for ages, since around the Civil War, I think. Don was a hard man. He woke early, stood on his feet all day, drank awful coffee, and cussed like a mildly drunk sailor. He spent all day every day tossing around fifty-pound boxes of nails and repairing lawn mower engines. If you made a mistake around Don, he let you know it by saying lots of words that weren't said around my homeschooling house. He smelled of sweat, grease, and unhappiness. I rarely saw him happy. I frequently heard him complain and curse. I rarely heard him laugh. But Don didn't know Jesus, and so I wouldn't expect him to be happy.

Unfortunately, many people who do know Jesus are also very unhappy. If you were to wiretap their daily conversations, you wouldn't hear much gratefulness, joy, or encouragement. You would hear the steady drip of complaining, whining, grumbling. You wouldn't see many smiles or hear much laughter.

These folks go to church and small group and talk about the joy of the Lord. About being a shining light, a witness for Christ. And then they go to work and cast shadows. They walk around in a semi-gloom, always ready for a good complaining session, ready to get things off their chest. These people don't have a lot of success in inviting people to church. After all, who wants to go to church with Captain Gloom?

In 1 Thessalonians 5:16–18 Paul says, "Rejoice always, pray without ceasing, give thanks in all circumstances; for this is the will of God in Christ Jesus for you." God calls us to constant rejoicing, and he's given us every reason to rejoice. The gospel gives us every reason to rejoice. Forgiveness of sins gives us every reason to rejoice. Calling God "Father" gives us every reason to rejoice. Knowing Jesus, the source of all joy, peace, and life, gives us every reason to rejoice. We always have reason to rejoice and never have reason to complain.

Psalm 100:1–2 says, "Make a joyful noise to the LORD, all the earth! Serve the LORD with gladness! Come into his presence with singing!" Gladness matters to God. When we serve him with gladness, we are in effect saying, "I'm so glad to be a follower of Jesus. There is no Master I would rather serve. Following Jesus brings me so much joy." It's not enough to simply be a soldier in the Lord's army, glumly fulfilling our Christian duty. That dishonors God. We don't serve a drill-sergeant God. We serve a God who gives fullness of joy, who sacrificed his Son so that we might have joy, who invites us to taste and see that he is good. God is honored by joyful, glad, complaint-free service.

Complaining sucks the joy out of life. The complainer can't even enjoy the good things he has. Again quoting Thomas Watson, "Discontent is a fretting humor which dries the brain, wastes the spirits, and corrodes and eats out the comfort of life. Discontent makes a man so that he does not enjoy what he possesses."[2]

When we complain, we portray God as a joyless Scrooge in the sky, a miserable master who has no time for happiness. We show our neighbors and friends that followers of Jesus are scowling, joyless drips who follow a joyless master.

ME, DON, AND JESUS

I'm not sure where Don is today. I haven't talked to him in over ten years, and he recently sold his hardware store. My guess is that unless Jesus took hold of him, he's still an unhappy person.

And apart from the power of Jesus I would be just like Don, a cranky man with a beef against life. But slowly, little by little, Jesus is transforming me. I don't want to be like Don. I don't want to dishonor God by complaining. I love God. No one has been kinder to me or taken better care of me. No one has loved me like he has. I don't want to complain against this God whom I love. I don't want to slander the One who has been so kind to me. I serve a wonderful Master, and I want my words to bring honor to him.

STOP—THINK—DO

1. Do you see complaining as a serious sin? Why or why not?

2. Write down just a few of the ways that God has blessed you. When you complain, what are you saying about the way that God treats you?

3. Read Romans 8:28. Why does this Scripture leave no room for complaining?

4. Why is complaining a form of accusing God?

5. Would you be characterized more by thankfulness or complaining? What is one step you can take to grow in thankfulness?

10

COUNT YOUR BLESSINGS— LITERALLY

The phrase "count your blessings" has always struck me as cheesy and horribly insincere. People seem to break it out at the worst times. When someone tells me that a water pipe burst in his basement and ruined half of his worldly possessions, he doesn't want me to tell him that it could be worse and that he should count his blessings. He wants me to tell him about a good Christian missionary plumber who feels called to do all his work for free. He wants me to say, "I happen to have this entire week off from work, so I'll be over every night to help you clean up." When I say, "Count your blessings," he probably feels like saying, "How about you count my blessings, and while you're doing that I'll go take some of your blessings." I've never been a fan of telling people to do a blessing count, particularly when their lives are falling apart.

But in recent months my perspective has begun to shift. I've started to realize that I'm rich beyond most people's wildest dreams. That I enjoy more material blessings in one day than most people enjoy in a lifetime. That for reasons I can't explain, God allowed me to be born in one of the richest countries in the world and to enjoy its benefits. If I had received the blessings of the gospel and nothing else, I would have enough to be content for eternity. But I've received much, much more.

Discontentment happens when I don't have what I want.

Contentment happens when I realize that I have so much more than I deserve.

So for a few moments, let's put all our desires on hold and ponder the great mountain of blessings that we already have. James 1:17 says, "Every good gift and every perfect gift is from above, coming down from the Father of lights with whom there is no variation or shadow due to change." We have received so many good gifts. Let's stop obsessing about what we want and start marveling at all that God has given us.

LIFE

Last night thousands of people entered eternity. Heart monitors flat-lined. Lungs ceased pulling in air. Brains that were once incredibly active went silent.

Yet today I live. Through the night my lungs continued to suck air, and my heart continued to push blood through my body. God gave me yet another day to serve him, enjoy my family, watch a movie, drink coffee, play football, laugh with friends, and read a good book. I have one more day to prepare for eternity, one more day to store up treasures for that final day.

Hebrews 1:3 says of Jesus, "He is the radiance of the glory of God and the exact imprint of his nature, and he upholds the universe by the word of his power." Jesus keeps the universe and the solar system and my heart running by his word. Jesus could bring my life to a close with a simple word. So why did he allow me to live today? Thousands of people didn't wake up this morning. Some died in their sleep, some died of heart attacks or car crashes, some died of malaria, and some died of AIDS. Some people could feel death stalking them. Others had no idea that they would die. Countless funerals are occurring today. Why isn't mine one of them?

Life is a precious gift from God. He doesn't owe me a minute or a breath. Yet this morning I'm alive. God sustained me through the night and gave me at least one more day to enjoy.

HEALTH

I have a body that works reasonably well. My fingers are intact. Both of my eyes and ears work properly. My legs allow me to run and jump, and all of my ligaments are still pulling on the appropriate joints and muscles. I'm not confined to a bed or dependent on crutches.

I don't understand why God has allowed me to be so healthy. In her book *When God Weeps* Joni Eareckson Tada tells of meeting a woman in the slums of Africa:

> When the flap [of the woman's tent] dropped behind me, a dozen slum-street noises were muffled. My eyes would now do most of the learning. He [an African pastor] held his flashlight high, spotlighting a young woman with hair and skin as black as the shadows. She had no hands. Splayed beneath her on the straw mat were stick-thin legs. These did not hold my gaze. I had seen the alleys full of people who, from polio, or amputation, had stubs for hands or callused stumps for feet. All of them, homeless. Quadriplegics, like me, don't survive in Ghana, equatorial west Africa, let alone on the sidewalks of this miserable pesthole in the capital of Accra—only disabled people who are strong enough to fend for themselves on the streets. Streets wet with urine and rotting garbage.[1]

Why are my hands still attached to my arms? Why am I able to walk instead of being confined to a wheelchair? Why do my eyes still work? Why hasn't leprosy rotted the skin off my body? Because God has been incredibly kind to me. For some reason God has allowed me to have a healthy body and access to health care. Not because I'm better than anyone else but because God is merciful.

Any measure of health that we experience is a gift from God. It's pure mercy. Can we exercise? A gift. Can we see? A gift. Can we walk on our own strength? A gift. Can we get out of bed on our own power? A gift.

Millions of people would be thankful for the ability to climb out of bed. I'm able to run, play with my daughter, shoot a basketball, go skiing, and see the sunrise. Am I thankful for these gifts?

FOOD

I have a pantry and a refrigerator that are packed with food. If the earth was hit by an enormous meteor, leading to worldwide food shortages, I could easily survive for weeks on the food that is currently in my house. Three blocks from my house is a grocery store. In that store alone is enough food to feed thousands of people. If I suddenly have a craving for a salami log, I can have one in my possession in twenty minutes or less.

I eat three full meals a day and multiple snacks in between those meals. The minute I'm hungry I can walk into my kitchen, rummage through my pantry, and find something to satisfy me. I don't have to wait in line or hope that I'll have enough money to purchase food. I always have a full fridge and a full stomach.

I also have enough food to feed my little girl. Sometimes she decides that she really doesn't like what we're eating for dinner, and I actually have the option of giving her something else.

Every day thousands of people die from malnutrition. They die a slow, hollow, withering death. Little children walk around with distended stomachs and vacant stares. A bowl of rice and a cup of clean water is enough to satisfy them. If they could see my pantry, they would be startled at the abundance of food, and they would marvel that I ever complain of not having anything to eat. Millions live on the bitter edge of starvation. I live in the midst of abundance.

In 1 Timothy 6:8 Paul says, "if we have food and clothing, with these we will be content." God has given me much more than food and clothing. Compared to most of the world, I feast every day. I eat more in a week than many people eat in a month. I really do live like a king.

Why am I able to give my daughter a bowl of Cheerios every

single morning? Why am I able to eat a pre-bedtime snack of cheese and crackers? I don't go to bed with a hollow stomach, wondering how I'm going to feed myself or my family. God has been so kind to me. He's blessed me lavishly, abundantly, in ridiculous, overflowing measure. The hunger of the world rebukes my complaining. Let me never complain again of a bad meal. Let me never again utter the words, "There's nothing to eat in this house." God has blessed me with mountains of food.

SHELTER AND POSSESSIONS

An old mattress. A piece of disintegrating corrugated aluminum. Rusty chicken-wire fencing. Mud. Thatch. Rotting wood. These are the materials used to build many houses around the world. I've seen it with my own eyes in Mexico.

Water for drinking and bathing comes from bacteria-infested pools. Children play with a soccer ball made of bundled rags. Hordes of people are slowly assassinated by malaria-carrying mosquitoes because they can't afford to put mosquito netting around their beds.

I, on the other hand, live in a three-bedroom palace. Every morning I take a steaming hot shower in water so clean it glistens. I walk across my clean ceramic tile floor and accidentally kick a toy that my daughter left out. She has mountains of toys. When the house gets cold, my 90 percent efficiency furnace kicks in, blasting hot air through the vents and throughout the house. But even if a small rodent crawled into the furnace and caused it to melt down, I'd be fine. I'd simply add an additional layer of clothing from my full closet.

When my body wears down, I collapse onto my couch and start stabbing at the television with the remote. There are so many channels I don't know what to watch. If I get bored with television I can grab one of the hundreds of books that I own. Sometimes, if one of my favorite books has gotten particularly beat up, I'll go out and buy a second copy. Without a second thought.

I drive to work in my car, which I own. The bank can't squeeze another penny out of me for that vehicle. The muffler has a hole in it, which makes the car sound like a Cessna airplane when I start it. But I'm not too worried about it. I have breathing room in my budget to get it fixed.

LIVING IN LUXURY

Do you get the picture? Compared to most of the world, I'm a king living in a palace. I'm surrounded by luxury. I have more than I need, more than anyone needs. And I still can't figure out why God has blessed me. Why do I have these blessings and most people don't? Why is my little girl healthy when many little girls are so weak from malnutrition that they can't even stand? Why do I have clean water that isn't full of horrible parasites? Why is a broken bone a minor inconvenience for me and a catastrophe for someone living in Africa? I can only come to one conclusion: God has been very kind to me.

And I can only see one appropriate response: gratefulness to God.

I want the kind of gratefulness to God that creates contentment in my heart. I may not have everything my heart desires, but I have more than most people desire, and I have infinitely more than I deserve.

I want gratefulness to God that shuts my complaining mouth. I complain about things that would cause most people to rejoice. I have a car that can break down. I have a house that needs repairs. I have a computer that occasionally goes spastic. I have access to health care when my normally healthy body gets sick. I throw things into the garbage that people in other countries would treasure. The blessings I've received leave no room for complaining in my life.

The great Puritan Matthew Henry was once robbed of his wallet. After pondering the incident, he wrote the following words in his diary:

> I thank Thee first because I was never robbed before; second, because although they took my purse they did not take my life;

third, because although they took my all, it was not much; and fourth because it was I who was robbed, and not I who robbed.

Being held up and robbed probably didn't rank high on the enjoyable experience scale for Matthew Henry. But rather than give in to the temptation to complain, he paused for a moment and took stock of all that he been given. He had never been robbed before. He was still alive. They took all he had, but it wasn't very much. And by the grace of God he was the one being robbed and not the other way around. Matthew Henry counted his blessings, which in turn stopped him from complaining.

While preaching a sermon, Charles Spurgeon said, "I have heard of some good old woman in a cottage, who had nothing but a piece of bread and a little water. Lifting up her hands, she said as a blessing, 'What! All this, and Christ too?'"[2] The old woman understood that in Christ she had everything and that everything in addition to Christ was pure blessing. I have far more than a piece of bread and a little water. Every time I step into the shower or enjoy a cup of coffee or watch a football game, I want my heart to be singing, "All this, and Christ too?"

STOP—THINK—DO

1. Are you more aware of the things that you want or the blessings that you've been given?

2. Given all the blessings you've received, how do you think your complaining affects God?

3. What are some practical steps you can take to cultivate gratefulness for the blessings God has brought to you?

4. How was Matthew Henry able to give thanks to God just after being robbed?

5. In light of God's generosity to you, is there one way you can help those who truly do live in poverty?

11

THE FURNACE OF SUFFERING

This chapter doesn't begin with a joke or clever illustration or mildly amusing personal story. In fact, I'm not sure where to begin, because this chapter is about finding contentment in the midst of suffering.

I've suffered very little in my life. No chronic illnesses, no tragic deaths, no world-shattering events. Yet.

But I've watched many people suffer in awful ways. There are men and women in my church who have endured, and are enduring, fiery, world-twisting trials. Chronic arthritis that puts hot nails between every joint. Extreme, unrelenting, chest-squeezing financial pressure. The slow, fierce creep of Alzheimer's disease. The persistent joy-sucking gloom of clinical depression. Terminal brain cancer.

These friends are my heroes, because in the midst of suffocating suffering they still honor God. They don't curse God. They don't hate God. Yes, they weep. Yes, they have questions. Yes, they have some days when it hurts to get out of bed. But they praise the Lord anyway. They bless the God who gives and takes away. They set a breathtaking example for me to follow.

This chapter is for my heroes. For those of you who are following Christ through high waters and hot flames. For those of you who are living martyrs, testifying to the power of Christ as the fire licks your feet.

I don't want to give you pat, trite answers. I don't want to tell you just to trust in God and everything will be okay. I simply want to connect you to the God who is bigger than your sufferings and who fully understands what I don't. I want to connect you to the only person who can carry you through and give you contentment in the midst of suffering. I want to connect you to Jesus.

GOD UNDERSTANDS

I don't understand what you are going through. I don't understand the depths of sorrow you've endured or the racking pain that jolts you awake at 2:00 A.M. I can't fathom the loneliness that plagues you after the death of a loved one. I can't relate to the bone-crushing weariness that comes with continually caring for an ill family member. I've never had to lay in a blacked-out room with a cool cloth on my head, waiting for a pulsing migraine to pass.

You've had people tell you that they understand what you're going through, but until they endure it they don't really know. Their words, while well-meaning, ring hollow. So I won't pretend to understand. I'll weep with you, but I won't try to convince you that I get it.

There is one person, however, who truly does understand your suffering. There is one person who has been swallowed by sorrow, and engulfed by pain, and overwhelmed by blackness. Isaiah 53:3 describes Jesus by saying, "He was despised and rejected by men; a man of sorrows, and acquainted with grief."

Jesus, God in flesh, the maker of the world, was a man of sorrows. His life was bathed in sorrow. He didn't have a few sorrows sprinkled into his life, like herbs to flavor a meal. He was "a man of sorrows." The Light of the World lived in gloom.

He encountered rejection wherever he went. And this wasn't cold-shoulder, "let's not talk for a while" rejection. People wanted to kill him. They wanted to throw rocks at him until he died. They wanted to push him off a cliff. Jesus found himself consistently "despised and rejected," with the shadow of death always pressing down on him.

The Holy One had his name smeared in every way imaginable. People called Jesus a bastard and his mother a whore (John 8:41). When he hung out with sinners, the religious leaders called him a thirsty-fingered drunk and a glutton (Luke 7:34). When Jesus rescued people from demons, they said he was in league with Satan (Matt. 12:24). When he healed people on the Sabbath, they accused him of being a pagan lawbreaker (John 9:16). His own family thought he was a joke (John 7:5).

After three years of being slandered, smeared, accused, rejected, mocked, and threatened, everything came to a head. The religious leaders arrested Jesus and put him through a rigged trial. They spit on him and slapped him and mocked him, daring the Almighty to strike back. The King of kings stood there, coated with the spit of others and his own blood. The one worshiped by angels was humiliated and shamed.

Then Jesus was handed over to the Romans, who were much more experienced in the torture and execution business. Pontius Pilate thoroughly cross-examined Jesus and came to the conclusion that he was innocent. Of course he would come to that conclusion. But the religious leaders were on a death crusade and would be happy with nothing less than a lifeless body. And so Pilate threw Jesus to the wolves. Did the angels of heaven scream at the injustice? Did they plead with God to let them go down and decapitate the wicked and rescue Jesus? Were they shocked at the degradation of their King?

The Roman soldiers wanted to have some fun with Jesus before they killed him. First they scourged him, ruining his back with a whip. Pieces of bone and metal were embedded into the whip, and each stroke tore Jesus' muscles and nerves and tendons. By the time they were done, Jesus' entire torso was a gaping wound. Then over a hundred men swarmed around him, ripping off his clothes, cursing him, laughing and leering at him, spitting on him, dressing him in a costume, and then slamming thorns onto his head. Did Jesus throw up from the pain?

Finally the Romans nailed Jesus to a cross. Metal nails plunged into the hands and feet of God, and he hung suspended between heaven and earth. As he hung upon the cross, hell descended upon Jesus. God the Father unleashed his hatred of sin upon his Son. The Light of the World was engulfed in horrific blackness as Jesus became our sin (2 Cor. 5:21). God punished Jesus as if he were the rapist, the pedophile, the drunkard, the adulterer, the religious prig, the arrogant fool, and the self-righteous.

The Son of God has suffered more than any person in history. He understands pain and sorrow and blackness in a way that none of us ever will. And because he has suffered more than anyone else, he is perfectly suited to help those who are suffering.

Hebrews 2:18 says, "For because he himself has suffered when tempted, he is able to help those who are being tempted." Jesus is able to give real help to you in the midst of your suffering. Why? Because he endured unbelievable suffering. The Son of God truly understands what you are going through. He understands physical pain. He understands loneliness and abandonment. He understands the dark night of your soul. He experienced it all and is able to give grace to you in your suffering.

Run to Jesus and unburden yourself at his feet. Lay your griefs upon his chest and let him bear the weight. Let the Man of Sorrows strengthen you in your sorrow. He can prop your head when you are suffocating in sadness. He can strengthen you when you are emotionally and spiritually spent. Call out to him for light in the midst of darkness. Call out to him for strength in the midst of weakness. The one who suffered knows exactly what you need.

The counsel and care of others, while helpful and necessary, is not the ultimate solution. Jesus is the one who gives strength and contentment in the midst of suffering. Cling tightly to Jesus, who already has you in his invincible grip.

GOD CARES

My two-year-old daughter is one of my greatest joys in life. The affection I feel for her is deeper than I can put into words. I treasure her.

I delight in her. I love spending time with her and playing with her and laughing with her and chasing her around our living room. And my heart breaks when she suffers.

When she's sick, my heart is filled with compassion toward her. I want to sit with her, rock with her, let her feel my arms wrapped around her little body, and tell her that it's going to be okay. I give her special treatment, and my ears are especially tuned to her cries. If she wakes up crying in the middle of the night, I'm quickly by her side, comforting her and attending to her needs.

My intense affection and compassion for my daughter are the faintest reflection of God's affection and compassion for us. Psalm 103:13 says, "As a father shows compassion to his children, so the LORD shows compassion to those who fear him." God has gone to incredible lengths to make us his children. He killed his Son so that we could be forgiven. He hunted us down so that we could be adopted. He embraced us in our filth so that we could be made clean. God is our Father, and his heart burns with affection for us.

In his book *Knowing God*, J. I. Packer says the following about our adoption into God's family:

> Adoption is a family idea, conceived in terms of love, and viewing God as father. In adoption, God takes us into His family and fellowship, and establishes us as His children and heirs. Closeness, affection and generosity are at the heart of the relationship. To be right with God the judge is a great thing, but to be loved and cared for by God the father is greater.[1]

Because of justification, we are right with God the Judge. Because of adoption, we are treasured by God the Father. Closeness, affection, and generosity are at the heart of our relationship with God. We are deeply loved and cared for by God our Father. God brings us close to himself and is filled with affection and generosity for us.

When you suffer, God feels it. He feels deep tenderness toward you as you lie in bed for the third straight day with a blinding headache. He feels compassion toward you as you weep with loneliness at night. In Psalm 56:8 David cries to God, "You have kept count of my tossings; put my tears in your bottle. Are they not in your book?" God sees every tear that you shed and the tossing and turning that takes place in your soul. He doesn't turn a cold shoulder to your suffering. He's not a football coach who tells you to suck it up and put some ice on it. Your suffering matters to God. Deeply.

When my daughter is suffering, I *want* her to come to me. I want to take care of her. I would be broken if she thought I didn't care about her suffering. I'm her father.

In the midst of suffering you can run to your Father. He wants you to come near and feel his care. He wants you to give him the cares and anxieties that suck the breath out of your chest (1 Pet. 5:7). His ears are attentive to your every cry and whimper (Ps. 34:17).

To try and muscle your way through suffering is insanity. You have an infinite, almighty Father who is full of compassion toward you. The path to contentment in suffering goes through the Savior who suffered for you to your Father who is compassionate toward you.

GOD ALLOWS

We now wade into a deep, deep mystery. If God is all-powerful and is a loving Father, why does he allow you to suffer? I'm not going to attempt to fully answer that question for two reasons. First, there are already numerous, very helpful books written by men and women who are more godly than me and who have suffered more than I have. Read them for the good of your soul. I would especially recommend *When God Weeps: Why Our Sufferings Matter to the Almighty* by Joni Eareckson Tada and Steve Estes and *If God Is Good: Faith in the Midst of Suffering and Evil* by Randy Alcorn.

Second, to answer that deep question requires much more than a few paragraphs.

So instead of answering the question directly, I simply want to remind you of a few things that you probably already know. I want to point you to the God who is standing with you in the midst of the hurricane.

Suffering is often a mystery. We're not taken behind the curtain to see all the glorious things that God is accomplishing through our suffering. It's hard to make sense of heart attacks and brain hemorrhages and miscarriages. It's hard to see clearly through the buzzing pain that descends upon us. But we do know that God doesn't waste a drop of suffering. He isn't a masochist who enjoys inflicting pain upon people. Every bit of your suffering—every heartache, every arthritic joint, every sleepless night—is being used for your good. No exceptions.

Romans 8:28 makes it clear that God is harnessing all your suffering for your good and his glory: "And we know that for those who love God all things work together for good, for those who are called according to his purpose." You're not God's test lab rat. He's not experimenting on you. God doesn't play games with suffering. Every ounce of your suffering is being shaped and molded by your Father to do you good and to bring him glory. It's all for good and all for glory.

This truth is brutally difficult to grasp in the emergency room, sitting amidst a nest of tubes. As the doctor jams yet another needle into your arm. As different machines keep your body from collapsing upon itself.

But ultimately the machines don't sustain you. You're in the gentle hand of your Father, and so are the tubes and needles and hissing machines. God brings goodness and glory out of the hurricane. Contentment happens when we rest in the gentle hand of God in the midst of our sufferings.

Second Corinthians 4:16–18 says, "So we do not lose heart. Though our outer self is wasting away, our inner self is being renewed day by day. For this light momentary affliction is preparing for us an eternal weight of glory beyond all comparison, as we look not to the things that are seen but to the things that are unseen." Commenting on this passage, Ligon Duncan says:

> You couldn't bear the glory that God has in store for you, unless you had been held up by God in your affliction in this life. The apostle Paul is telling you that your suffering is not just for now. It is not just for maturity in Christ—though it is for that. It is not just for godliness—though it is for that too. It is not just so that you'll prize Christ now, or for the edification of the body—though it is for those good purposes as well. Your suffering prepares you for a glory that you cannot even comprehend. If you were not being held up by God in your affliction now, you could not bear the glory that He is going to bestow upon you.[2]

Some of you are wasting away outwardly. Your body is failing you. Walking feels like death. Breathing is like trying to suck air through a sponge. Outwardly you're disintegrating.

But inwardly God is doing something beautiful. He's preparing you to enjoy heaven. He's preparing you to receive glorious, eternal, jaw-dropping blessings that you couldn't receive unless you suffered. When you see these blessings you'll weep and laugh with joy. You'll marvel at how such blessings could come out of such suffering. And you'll bless your Father, who prepared you to enjoy these blessings.

Contentment happens when, through faith, you see the treasure waiting for you.

COURAGE, DEAR HEART

The Voyage of the Dawn Treader by C. S. Lewis is one of my favorite books of all time. It tells the story of Prince Caspian, Edmund, Lucy, and Eustace and the adventures they have together aboard the ship *The Dawn Treader*. At one point in the book the ship's crew spots a great black mass in front of them. As soon as the ship enters the blackness, it becomes apparent that something evil is in the air. Those on the ship hear a voice crying out for help, and they pull aboard a trembling old man who tells them that this is the place where nightmares become reality.

Soon everyone begins to see their worst nightmares appear before them. Horrible noises fill the air, and the oppressive blackness throws everyone into a panic.

"We'll never get out!" the sailors begin to scream.

In desperation Lucy cries out to Aslan, the Great Lion and Son of the Emperor.

Lucy leant her head on the edge of the fighting-top and whispered, "Aslan, Aslan, if ever you loved us at all, send us help now." The darkness did not grow any less, but she began to feel a little—a very, very little—better. "After all, nothing has really happened to us yet," she thought.

"Look!" cried Rynelf's voice hoarsely from the bows. There was a tiny speck of light ahead, and while they watched a broad beam of light fell from it upon the ship. It did not alter the surrounding darkness, but the whole ship was lit up as if by searchlight. Caspian blinked, stared round, saw the faces of his companions all with wild, fixed expressions. Everyone was staring in the same direction: behind everyone lay his black, sharply edged shadow.

Lucy looked along the beam and presently saw something in it. At first it looked like a cross, then it looked like an aeroplane, then it looked like a kite, and at last with a whirring of wings it was right overhead and was an albatross. It circled three times round the mast and then perched for an instant on the crest of the gilded dragon at the prow. It called out in a strong sweet voice what seemed to be words though no one understood them. After that it spread its wings, rose, and began to fly slowly ahead, bearing a little to starboard. Drinian steered after it not doubting that it offered good guidance. But no one except Lucy knew that as it circled the mast it had whispered to her, "Courage, dear heart," and the voice, she felt sure, was Aslan's, and with the voice a delicious smell breathed in her face.

In a few moments the darkness turned into a grayness ahead, and then, almost before they dared to begin hoping, they had shot out into the sunlight and were in the warm, blue world again.[3]

To those of you who are battling illness, "Courage." To those of you who are in the gloom of depression, "Courage." To those of you who are wondering if you'll make it though another day, "Courage." To those of you who sob yourself to sleep at night, "Courage."

To those of you who are suffering, the Lord would say, "Courage, dear heart."

STOP—THINK—DO

1. Read Isaiah 53. How does Jesus' suffering encourage you in the midst of your suffering?

2. Read Hebrews 2:18. Why does Jesus' suffering make him perfectly suited to help you in your suffering?

3. Are you aware of God's deep, fatherly love for you? What keeps you from believing that God deeply loves you?

4. How can you grow in your awareness of God's love for you?

5. Are you ever tempted to believe that your suffering is pointless? What do Romans 8:28 and 2 Corinthians 4:16–18 have to say to this?

12

THE END OF TEARS

I think I'm cursed. Not the Hollywood kind of curse, which can be solved with a dehydrated monkey head, a vial of goat's blood, and the hair of a pregnant llama. I'm talking about a real, flesh-and-blood, dark and sinister curse.

Point in case: my new house. Remember how I said at the beginning of the book that I didn't own a house? Well, in God's kindness things have changed. In the course of writing this book, I was able to buy a house.

But before we could move in, the house needed some work. Every wall needed a new coat of paint, and the cupboards needed a serious overhaul. It was during these minor renovations that I discovered the curse.

Weird, unexplainable things started happening. The fresh paint on one wall began bubbling, as if the wall had developed a terrible case of junior high school acne. It took hours to lance all the bubbles and get a wall with a clean complexion. The freshly painted cupboards looked great until I started putting the doors back on. Suddenly nothing lined up. Doors wouldn't close or they would overlap onto other doors.

Also, old, decomposing carpet that should have come up with a gentle tug was held in place by a mysterious, all-powerful glue.

This was strange, and frustrating. It was as if an evil spirit was trying to disrupt everything I did. As if I and my house were under an oppressive darkness that caused all my best efforts to be futile. As if, well, as if I was cursed.

And as it turns out, I really am cursed. And so are you. In Genesis 3 God pronounces his judgment upon the earth and all its inhabitants. Notice what he says to Adam and Eve:

> To the woman he said, "I will surely multiply your pain in childbearing; in pain you shall bring forth children. Your desire shall be for your husband, and he shall rule over you." And to Adam he said, "Because you have listened to the voice of your wife and have eaten of the tree of which I commanded you, 'You shall not eat of it,' cursed is the ground because of you; in pain you shall eat of it all the days of your life; thorns and thistles it shall bring forth for you; and you shall eat the plants of the field. By the sweat of your face you shall eat bread, till you return to the ground, for out of it you were taken; for you are dust, and to dust you shall return." (Gen. 3:16–19)

Because Adam sinned, women scream and sweat and have epidurals during childbirth. Because Adam sinned, men and women experience frustration and futility in their work. Thumbs get mashed by hammers. Cabinets are hung crookedly. Food burns. Copy machines self-destruct. Unmet deadlines leave us gasping and grasping.

The entire earth is under the judgment of God. Things are not as God originally intended. Death stalks us all, waiting for us at busy intersections and beside hospital beds. Relationships are shattered by sin, and the creation itself wages war against us. Tornadoes and tsunamis rip through communities and lives, leaving corpses and weeping children in their wake. The good world that God originally created is now a smoking, charred shell of what it once was.

This puts us who are Christians in a difficult spot. We now live in tension, caught between two worlds. We're called to live contented, grateful lives while on the earth. But ultimately this world isn't our home. As Randy Alcorn says, "You are made for a person and a place. Jesus is the person. Heaven is the place."[1] We're called to always be content, yet never truly comfortable, always joyful, yet always longing.

Lasting contentment on earth is the result of fixing our eyes on heaven. If we're going to be content in the midst of prolonged suffering, we need to keep our eyes on the place where suffering finally ends. If we're going to press through loneliness and poverty and sickness, we need to look to the one who will wipe all our tears away.

This chapter is not a theology of heaven. Others, like Randy Alcorn, have already done that. I simply want to connect the dots between the glories of what's to come and our current battle for contentment. In order to do that, we need to spend a few moments marveling at the person and place for which we were made.

MADE FOR A PERSON

Why is it that we're always forming and joining clubs? Old guys who smell like tobacco and aftershave get together to drink beer and play poker. Women join bridge clubs, date groups, and cooking clubs. If you're a boy, you join the Boy Scouts and learn to do things like tie knots and earn merit badges. If you're a girl, you join the Girl Scouts and learn to sell cookies (I'm sure they do more, but since I wasn't a Girl Scout I don't know). Everyone wants fellowship and desires to be a part of something. Why?

Part of the reason is that God created us for fellowship with himself and others. Our longing to experience community is a good, God-given desire. Man shouldn't be alone. And so God gave Adam fellowship—first with God, then with Eve. This fellowship was good and perfect until sin entered the scene.

Now all relationships are fractured and splintered. Sin cuts us off from relationship with God. Because God is holy and we're sinful, we're excluded from the presence of God. Sin also drives a wedge between us and others. Not content to wait until marriage, singles engage in sex outside of marriage. Couples engage in verbal gunfights and physical fistfights. Widows and widowers feel cut off and isolated. Sin wreaks havoc with our relationships.

When someone is saved by God, the fractured relationships begin to heal. We have access to God through the blood of Jesus. Our relationships with others, which were once rooted in piggish selfishness, are now rooted in Christ. People we once despised, we now love. The gospel changes everything.

But things are still not as God intended. Our sin still clouds and harms our experience of fellowship with God. Singles are still haunted by loneliness. Couples long for greater intimacy with each other and closer friendships in the church. Our relationships are still imperfect at best.

Through Christ who strengthens us, we can be content in our loneliness and disjointed relationships. But our longings for relationships should also remind us that this world is not our final resting place. In Christ we can be truly content while on this earth, but we'll never be fully satisfied. The day of total, complete, and ultimate satisfaction is still coming. The day we see Jesus Christ face-to-face and look into the eyes of our Savior, we'll say, "Now I'm truly satisfied."

In Psalm 27:4 David says, "One thing have I asked of the LORD, that will I seek after: that I may dwell in the house of the LORD all the days of my life, to gaze upon the beauty of the LORD and to inquire in his temple." David was obsessed. Preoccupied. Distracted. He asked God for one thing: to be in God's presence and look upon God's beauty. David wanted to see God and be with God. He knew that no earthly relationship could satisfy the deep longings of his heart.

C. S. Lewis said, "If I find in myself a desire which no experience in this world can satisfy, the most probable explanation is that I was made for another world."[2] In heaven, all our desires that could never be satisfied on earth will finally be met. We will look upon the face of Christ, and we will be in his immediate presence. First John 3:2 says, "Beloved, we are God's children now, and what we will be has not yet appeared; but we know that when he appears we shall be like him, because we shall see him as he is." In Revelation 5:6 John sees that all of heaven revolves around the Lamb who was slain. These passages indicate that we will look upon the very face of Jesus Christ, and when we see him, our knees will buckle and our mouths will fall open. We're not talking about floating around in an ethereal, heavenly mist and having a warm, Vicks VapoRub feeling inside. We're talking about really seeing the living Christ, the King of kings, the Savior, the one who makes the angels tremble and the demons cower.

Randy Alcorn says, "Not only will we see his face and live, but we will likely wonder if we ever lived before we saw his face!"[3] When we see Christ, we'll realize that all our earthly longings were really longings to see and be with Christ. When we look upon Jesus, the battle for contentment will come to an end, and we'll finally have all that we ever desired.

Have you ever been captivated by someone? You love being with her (or him), relaxing with her, laughing with her, and doing different activities with her. She makes everything fun, and time flies when you're hanging out with her. Heaven is captivated by Jesus, and we will be too. He makes everything exciting and glorious and vibrant.

Marriage isn't the ultimate. Deep friendships aren't the source of eternal joy. Being in heaven in the presence of the Father, Son, and Holy Spirit is the ultimate. Being face-to-face with and talking with, feasting with, and serving Jesus is the end-all. Throw away your ideas of a boring heaven with nothing to do. We're going to be with our Creator, the one who invented gladness and created fun. Heaven is going to be ringing with joy and laughter and excitement.

Jonathan Edwards said, "To go to heaven fully to enjoy God, is infinitely better than the most pleasant accommodations here. Fathers and mothers, husbands, wives, children, or the company of earthly friends are but shadows. But the enjoyment of God is the substance."[4]

Marriage is a wonderful gift from God. Friendships and children are sweet enjoyments from our Father. But if we stake our hope on them, we'll find that we've been chasing shadows.

Long-lasting, suffering-enduring contentment is only possible if we are regularly looking forward to the time when all our desires will be satisfied. We aren't going to be eternally unsatisfied. We aren't going to be fighting discontentment forever. Our everlasting joy is a breath away. God, the happiest person in the universe, is waiting for us.

Let's allow our current battles with discontentment to serve as reminders of heaven. When you feel lonely, pray that God would bring you a godly, attractive spouse. Then thank Jesus that someday your pangs of loneliness will be destroyed in the joy of his presence. When you long for deeper friendships, pray that God would give you close, Jesus-loving pals. Then turn your eyes to the day when all friendships will be perfected in Christ. When your heart is breaking because you can't conceive a baby, rest your broken heart in Jesus. Then, through the tears, look to the day when Jesus will wipe away every tear and say, "Well done, good and faithful servant." We fight the battle of contentment through Christ who strengthens us, but one day the battle will be over. Let's look ahead to that day.

MADE FOR A PLACE

It's time for a little honest confession: I don't like the artwork of Thomas Kinkade. I have trouble relating to what's going on in his pictures. Each painting seems to contain at least one of the following items: a bubbling brook, a perfectly constructed stone bridge, a snowy meadow, and a house so brightly lit that it must either be on fire or illuminated by 400-watt light bulbs.

These scenes painted by Kinkade don't match up with my experience. The creek running near my house has tires in it. The houses in my neighborhood are currently lit with hastily strung Christmas lights. The bridges in my area are made of cinder blocks and are usually covered with words not found in a homeschool classroom. Thomas Kinkade paintings feel a bit unreal to me.

But this doesn't seem to bother the millions of people who buy Kinkade paraphernalia by the boatload. Manufacturers have managed to fit his pictures onto almost every conceivable surface—paintings, magnets, mugs, Bible covers, canvas Jeep tops. What causes this frenzy? Why are there so many zealous Kinkade collectors?

My guess is that people are drawn to Kinkade's depiction of an ideal home, nestled away in the mountains next to a giggling brook. The paintings touch on our longing for a permanent, beautiful home.

This desire, like our desire for relationships, is from God. We were made for a place, a permanent, beautiful place. A place that makes Thomas Kinkade landscapes look like inner-city garbage dumps. That place is heaven.

When God originally created the earth, it was perfect, literally heaven on earth. God placed Adam and Eve in the Garden of Eden, and they lived in the essence of perfection. Picture the most beautiful nature hideaway you've ever seen, like *National Geographic* on steroids, and then multiply that by 1,000 percent. The gorgeous fruit trees were irrigated by cool rivers. A vast array of animals, insects, birds, and fish filled the garden and its rivers. Best of all, God himself walked in the garden. Adam and Eve lived in God's place, and they had intimate fellowship with God himself. This is the way God intended humans to live.

But God and sin cannot coexist, and so God drove Adam and Eve from the garden after they revolted against him. All people now live in exile, separated from God's presence and kept out of God's place. Sometimes we experience pangs of longing for Eden. We feel it when we arrive home after a long, out-of-state trip. We feel it during holidays when we're gathered around the dinner table with family. We feel it when we move from one house to another. We long for a permanent, stable, beautiful home.

Salvation through Jesus Christ is the first step toward our permanent home. Through the blood of Christ we've been adopted into God's family. We're no longer rebel orphans. We're God's children.

But we're still exiled from our home. We're still waiting for Jesus to return, to conquer his enemies, to reward his disciples, and to create the new heavens and the new earth. When that happens, we'll be home. We'll be in God's place, and it will be everything for which we always longed.

The earth, which is currently under the judgment of God, will be restored and renewed. Imagine what it's going to be like. Have you ever had the air stolen from your lungs by a gorgeous sunset? Have you looked up and up and up at a majestic, snowcapped mountain? Have you ever been swallowed up by the silence of a snowy wood? These are the faintest glimmers of what the new earth will be like. Everything will be restored and revived and made new. Evil will be purged from the earth. No more hurricanes, no more animal attacks, no more droughts. The beauty will be overwhelming. That's our home. That's where we're headed. We were made for that.

In 1 Corinthians 15:52–53 we're told that we'll receive new, imperishable, unbreakable bodies in the new earth: "For the trumpet will sound, and the dead will be raised imperishable, and we shall be changed. For this perishable body must put on the imperishable, and this mortal body must put on immortality." We'll receive bodies that don't perish, don't rot, don't get migraines, don't burn with arthritis, don't groan and creak when we climb out of bed in the morning. There will be no more cancer, no more miscarriages. Paralytics will sprint through the streets of the new Jerusalem, and those who are mute will finally sing the praise they've been storing up in their hearts. We'll have the bodies that God always intended us to have—perfect, vibrant, healthy, and without defect. There will be no crutches or back braces or ankle wraps in the new heaven and earth.

Boredom will not exist. Again quoting Randy Alcorn,

Our belief that Heaven will be boring betrays a heresy—that God is boring. There's no greater nonsense. Our desire for pleasure and the experience of joy comes directly from God's hand. He made our taste buds, adrenaline, sex drives, and the nerve endings that convey pleasure to our brains. Likewise, our imaginations and our capacity for joy and exhilaration were made by the very God we accuse of being boring. Are we so arrogant as to imagine that human beings came up with the idea of having fun?[5]

Because God is infinite and is the source of all pleasure (Ps. 16:11), heaven will be full of consistent, constant, guilt-free pleasure. We'll enjoy pleasures that we've never experienced on earth. Every pleasure we experience here is marred by the effects of sin. There is no such thing as unadulterated pleasure on earth. But there is in heaven.

Are you getting the picture? Heaven is the place for which we were made. All the delights we experience on earth are tiny echoes of the delights that pulse through heaven. Until we get to heaven, we are out of place.

Our citizenship in heaven has implications for how we live now. In 1 Peter 2:11 we read, "Beloved, I urge you as sojourners and exiles to abstain from the passions of the flesh, which wage war against your soul." We are "exiles" and "sojourners." We're aliens living in a foreign country, waiting to return to our homeland. This truth should compel us to make war against the sinful desires that make war against us. The prospect of our heavenly home should compel us to declare a holy war on the discontentment in our hearts.

When we're discontent, we're forgetting that heaven awaits us. Your futile house projects are a reminder that you're not home yet. Your constant battle with depression is a reminder that soon the gloom will lift. Your frustration with your job is a reminder that soon you'll be able to enjoy work as you were always meant to do. The strife that now rips at your family is a reminder that the King of Peace will soon destroy all sin.

Don't misunderstand. God wants us to experience contentment right now, in the midst of our house projects, depression, bad jobs, and strife. It's right and good to ask God to deliver us from each of these situations. But we can't stake our ultimate hope on deliverance because even if we're delivered from one trial, another will soon come our way. Our ultimate hope is in Jesus and in his place. When we're in heaven, the battle will be over. Contentment will not be a struggle. Peace, pleasure, and joy will take the day. But until that day we need to fight. Otherwise we'll find ourselves trying to make a home out of a place that was never intended to be our home. We'll pour our energy and time and thought into trying to find satisfaction on the earth rather than being content with what we have and looking forward to eternity.

HOMESICK FOR HEAVEN

So often discontentment is nothing more than longing for heaven. To quote Randy Alcorn one more time:

> Nothing is more often misdiagnosed than our homesickness for Heaven. We think that what we want is sex, drugs, alcohol, a new job, a raise, a doctorate, a spouse, a large-screen television, a new car, a cabin in the woods, a condo in Hawaii. What we really want is the person we were made for, Jesus, and the place we were made for, Heaven. Nothing less can satisfy us.[6]

If we're going to escape the Greener Grass Conspiracy, we must keep our eyes fixed on heaven. We can be content now because we know that very soon all of our longings will be satisfied. We can find happiness in the little we have on earth because we know of the riches that await us in heaven. We can contentedly endure suffering now because we know that soon Jesus will wipe away every tear.

This is my hope. I haven't yet learned to be content in all circumstances, but I'm fighting. I'm fighting because I know this isn't my home. I was made for Jesus, and I was made for heaven. And so were you.

STOP—THINK—DO

1. What is one way that you are currently experiencing the effects of living in a fallen world?

2. Would you say that you long for heaven? If not, why not? If so, what fuels your longing?

3. What does it mean that you were made for Jesus? How should that affect the way you live now?

4. What does it mean that you were made for heaven? How should that affect the way you live on earth?

5. Write down one or two ways that you are discontent. How do these desires actually reflect your homesickness for heaven?

NOTES

THE CONSPIRACY

1. If you are a normal, well-adjusted conspiracy theorist, please ignore the previous paragraph.

CHAPTER 1: WHY AM I SO UNHAPPY?

1. John Calvin, *Institutes of the Christian Religion*, ed. John T. McNeill, trans. Ford Lewis Battles (Louisville: Westminster, 1960), 108.

CHAPTER 3: SO WHAT AM I, A MONK?

1. Henry Bettenson, *Documents of the Christian Church*, second edition (London: Oxford University Press, 1963), 117–123.
2. Jeremiah Burroughs, *The Rare Jewel of Christian Contentment* (Carlisle, PA: Banner of Truth, 1964), 45.
3. This definition was adapted from Burroughs's book *The Rare Jewel of Christian Contentment*.
4. Iain Murray, *Jonathan Edwards: A New Biography* (Carlisle, PA: Banner of Truth, 1987), 327.
5. Thomas Watson, *The Art of Divine Contentment* (Morgan, PA: Soli Deo Gloria, 2001), 23.
6. Samuel Rodigast, "Whatever My God Ordains Is Right," 1676.

CHAPTER 4: I WORSHIP MY TELEVISION

1. Timothy Keller, *Counterfeit Gods: The Empty Promises of Money, Sex, and Power, and the Only Hope That Matters* (New York: Dutton, 2009), xix.
2. Ibid., 23–24.

CHAPTER 5: THE KING'S MADNESS

1. Remember the movie *Back to the Future*?
2. As quoted in John Piper, *The Purifying Power of Living by Faith in Future Grace* (Sisters, OR: Multnomah, 1995), 117.
3. Saint Augustine, *Confessions* (Oxford: Oxford University Press, 1998), 3.

CHAPTER 6: BLOODY CONTENTMENT

1. Joni Eareckson Tada and Steve Estes, *When God Weeps: Why Our Sufferings Matter to the Almighty* (Grand Rapids: Zondervan, 1997), 53–54.

2. John Piper, *God Is the Gospel: Meditations on God's Love as the Gift of Himself* (Wheaton: Crossway, 2005), 42.

3. John Piper's book *God Is the Gospel: Meditations on God's Love as the Gift of Himself* is a must-read when it comes to this subject. Most of my thoughts are borrowed from him.

4. Thomas Watson, *The Art of Divine Contentment* (Morgan, PA: Soli Deo Gloria, 2001), 96.

5. Ibid., 71.

6. Jeremiah Burroughs, *The Rare Jewel of Christian Contentment* (Carlisle, PA: Banner of Truth, 1964), 145.

7. *The Valley of Vision: A Collection of Puritan Prayers & Devotions*, ed. Arthur Bennett (Carlisle, PA: Banner of Truth, 1975), 8.

CHAPTER 7: SOME PEOPLE HAVE TO LEARN THE HARD WAY

1. I don't dislike speed-walkers. I just have a hard time not laughing when I see them wearing ankle weights and walking in that stiff, ostrich-like posture. Because, come on, that's funny. I look funny when I exercise, too.

2. *ESV Study Bible*, Introduction to Philippians (Wheaton: Crossway, 2008).

3. Acts 14:5–19.

4. See Acts 16:22.

5. 2 Corinthians 11:24.

6. Acts 27; 2 Corinthians 11:25.

7. Charles Spurgeon, *Morning and Evening* (Peabody, MA: Hendrickson, 1995), 94.

8. Thomas Watson, *The Art of Divine Contentment* (Morgan, PA: Soli Deo Gloria, 2001), 36.

9. I loved the homeschool choir. If any of my teachers are reading this, thanks for the hours you put into it.

CHAPTER 8: IN SEARCH OF THE SECRET

1. From http://www.thesecret.tv (accessed October 9, 2009).

2. Jeremiah Burroughs, *The Rare Jewel of Christian Contentment* (Carlisle, PA: Banner of Truth, 1964), 69.

3. Thomas Watson, *The Art of Divine Contentment* (Morgan, PA: Soli Deo Gloria, 2001), 22.

4. Ibid., 24.

5. Paul David Tripp, *Instruments in the Redeemer's Hands: People in Need of Change Helping People in Need of Change* (Phillipsburg, NJ: P&R, 2002), 54.

6. C. H. Spurgeon, "Sermon #346: All Sufficiency Magnified," *New Park Street Pulpit*, November 1860.

CHAPTER 9: EAT THE MEAT AND DIE

1. Thomas Watson, *The Art of Divine Contentment* (Morgan, PA: Soli Deo Gloria, 2001), 33.
2. Ibid., 26.

CHAPTER 10: COUNT YOUR BLESSINGS—LITERALLY

1. Joni Eareckson Tada and Steve Estes, *When God Weeps: Why Our Sufferings Matter to the Almighty* (Grand Rapids: Zondervan, 1997), 15.
2. Charles Spurgeon, *2200 Quotations from the Writings of Charles H. Spurgeon*, ed. Tom Carter (Grand Rapids: Baker, 1988).

CHAPTER 11: THE FURNACE OF SUFFERING

1. J. I. Packer, *Knowing God* (Downers Grove, IL: InterVarsity Press, 1973), 187–88.
2. Ligon Duncan and J. Nicholas Reid, *Does Grace Grow Best in Winter?* (Phillipsburg: P&R, 2009), 39–40.
3. C. S. Lewis, *The Voyage of the Dawn Treader* (New York: HarperCollins, 1980), 186–87.

CHAPTER 12: THE END OF TEARS

1. Randy Alcorn, *Heaven* (Wheaton: Tyndale House, 2004), 37.
2. C. S. Lewis, *Mere Christianity* (New York: Harper Collins, 1952), 136–37.
3. Alcorn, *Heaven*, 172.
4. Ibid., 185.
5. Ibid., 410.
6. Ibid., 166.

Do we have to stop so soon? Can't we continue this conversation? Stop over at my blog, The Blazing Center (www.theblazingcenter.com) and join with others as we talk about what it means to make Christ the glorious center of our lives. You'll also find lots of free stuff on the blog, like music, e-books, and Scripture memory tools. I'm also on Twitter (twitter.com/stephenaltrogge) and Facebook (facebook.com/StephenMAltrogge) and would love to connect with you there.

For information about the music I've produced in conjunction with Sovereign Grace Ministries, check out www.SovereignGraceMusic.com.

Thanks for reading!
Stephen